Your Life Design Blueprint

YOUR LIFE DESIGN BLUEPRINT

Discover your way to Passion, Purpose & Progress

ALBERT POLANCO

꞊ TABLE OF CONTENTS ꞊

Acknowledgements

I want to start this off first with absolute gratitude to each and every single person who supported my endeavor in writing my first of many books.

I want to thank my beautiful mother Carmen, for giving me life and having always done her best to show me her deep love for me.

And to her husband German, who takes care of my mother and loves her and brings joy into her life.

To my father Eliezer, for telling me how successful I would be as a little boy and sparking that entrepreneurial spirit in me at a very young age. We may not always see eye to eye but much of what I do and strive for has been influenced by you.

To my older brother Daniel, for listening to me ramble on and on about personal development and my ideas for this book. Often times helping me to figure things out by just talking about it.

To my brother from another mother and my business partner Ryan Reed, you have been an incredible friend, an inspiration to excellence and a source of wisdom and leadership. You have helped me and supported my ideas for this book. I have the best business partners anyone could ever hope for.

To Jimmy, for taking me out to lunch and teaching me about paying the price.

To Diana, for always being a light in my life your encouraging words over the last year have contributed to the improvement of my life and to my spiritual journey into mindfulness and meditation. Thank you, it has truly changed my life.

To all the people not listed here who have left me encouraging words and have supported this book from the very beginning I am grateful for you.

For all of my many mentors who have changed my life forever. Although most of you have spoken to me and shown me the way only through your books I am forever grateful for the value you have put out into the world that found its way to me.

To Jim Rohn, although you have been gone for many years your legacy, wisdom and message have inspired me to live out my absolute potential. Your teachings have guided me to a most exciting place in my journey.

For all of you, my heart is overflowing with the deepest feeling of gratitude. Thank you again, everyone who has influenced me in my life, the good and the bad, all of it has been incredibly valuable to me.

=1= Introduction

WHY I'M WRITING THIS BOOK

For most of my life, I have been a self-directed learner, being innately curious about *everything*. Before the advent of the internet, I would read as many books with pictures and explanations as I could. Since the creation of the internet, an unfathomable amount of information has become available at our fingertips.

With all this information overload, I found that returning to books could help me sift through much of the noise and discover massive shortcuts by learning from the trial and error of others. Many non-fiction and business-style books have incredibly valuable information that can open up doors that once seemed to be locked tight. In my opinion, there is one problem: many of these books are great at explaining theory, but lack a detailed and specific application method or system.

THEORY IS GREAT, BUT APPLICATION IS BETTER

I personally struggled with being able to take a high-level, potentially life-changing theory and put those concepts into action. I believe many others do too.

CREATE A SYSTEM

A sales trainer once told me, "Systems create freedom," and this quote has stuck with me. Through creating a simple predesigned system, I was able take a task that I had agonized over for many months and knock it out in one day. The power and sense of accomplishment I felt was immediate, and through all my other self-discovery experiences in my life, something clicked for me. In less than a week, I had the preliminary concepts and ideas I would use to create the "Life Design Blueprint."

TO INSPIRE AND HELP OTHERS LIKE MYSELF ACHIEVE THEIR DREAMS

From a very young age, I have always had this overwhelming feeling that there was a secret purpose and plan for my life. I felt I was destined to achieve great things. Maybe you have felt the same? As a child and young adult, I used to fantasize about being a superhero and making a massive impact on the world—but I didn't know what my superpower was yet. To be embarrassingly honest, I even had the feeling that I might not be from this planet. I was fascinated by the idea that we are made up of the elements of the stars—star children—and this idea inspired me. Some would call my thoughts delusions of grandeur while others would call them a burning passion to do big things.

Today, I believe that you should shoot for the stars, because even if you miss, at least you have a shot to reach the moon. If you only aim for the tree, you might trip on the curb, but you most likely won't reach any higher than the tree. We as human beings are capable of so much more than we ever imagined. Don't be afraid to dream and aim as high as possible. This book explains *how* to reach those goals that now may seem out of reach.

WHO I'M WRITING THIS BOOK FOR

This book is for self-directed and possibly self-educated people who are lifelong learners. This book is for you if you are the type of person who is always looking to improve and better yourself through finding mentors, reading books, listening to podcasts and audiobooks, or if you frequently look for training opportunities and other ways to actively improve your skills. If learning and improving excites you, then please keep reading.

This book is also for you if you are a creative dreamer who constantly jumps from project to project looking for ways to get the results you seek in life. If you can become good at nearly anything you have a deep interest in, or that allows you to be creative, then this book is for you. If you struggle severely with procrastination yet want to live a better life on your terms, you're in the right place.

This book is also for you if you understand the power that books have to transform your life but struggle with applying the ideas in many personal development books.

This is for you if you struggle with planning or don't like planning because you feel that life should be spontaneous. If you are the detailed and methodical planning type, I wrote this for you too.

If you already set goals and are ambitious but want to take things to the next level, I wrote this for you too.

Lastly, if you have big dreams for your life but just don't know where to start or how to get where you want to go, I wrote this for you.

I understand these personality types because, to varying degrees, I possess all of the traits I just described.

WHAT IS A LIFE DESIGN BLUEPRINT?

To put it simply, a Life Design Blueprint is a system that helps you to purposely design your life, make progress on reaching your goals, overcome obstacles, and keep your commitment to living the life you want for yourself and your family.

2
You Have to Pay the Price

One of my mentors that I look up to—we'll call him Jimmy—gave me the most bullshit-free piece of advice I could have ever asked for: "You have to pay the price." For whatever you want in life, you have to pay the price and do what it takes to succeed. It's very simple. This should be common sense, but as the saying goes, common sense ain't so common, right?

Jimmy fled from Vietnam under horrific conditions after witnessing brutal violence and suffering. At a very young age, he came to America with absolutely nothing, unable to speak the language and without a living soul to guide him or show him the way. Jimmy had the deck stacked against him early on in life. Fast forward to today: Jimmy is wealthy, healthy, successful and loved by his friends, family and community. In fact, he is not only a traveling pastor but also a financial advisor for a Fortune 100 company. How on earth did someone like Jimmy with all the odds against him become so successful? You know what Jimmy said to me when I asked him this very question? I remember waiting to hear a deeply profound and elegant explanation. He simply said, "I paid the price." That's it. At first, I thought, wow, that's it? How does that help me right now? What does that even mean? It took time for this to sink in for me, but it finally did. You see, Jimmy made sacrifices, worked hard, saved money, got an education and did all the things he thought were the right moves to lead him, over several decades, to success. Jimmy is a wonderful man and this one piece of advice still has meaning for me today. For anything I want in my life, I must pay the price.

You may be asking yourself: what is the price? We'll get to that later. For now, just remember that everything you want in life will cost you something. Maybe you're overestimating or underestimating what that cost will be, but more on this later. I want to introduce you to my other world-class mentors and some of the most profound lessons they've taught me.

3

13 Secrets I Learned from My World-Class Mentors

If you are anything like me and have a deep desire to achieve and succeed in life, then chances are you have a mentor or have been searching for mentors—people who can show you the way and maybe even give you an advantage in life. They can potentially speed up your path to success by years or even decades.

Whenever you hear big names like Tony Robbins, there is usually someone behind the scenes who helped to shape them. Many of Tony's fans know that Jim Rohn, a great and beloved motivational speaker, was his mentor. Microsoft's Bill Gates was mentored by one of the greatest financial minds of our time, Warren Buffett. Oprah Winfrey attributes much of her success to a celebrated author and poet, the late Maya Angelou. Actor Will Smith called Muhammad Ali his mentor and friend.

There is a common recurring theme among the most successful people on our planet: they seek out mentors that help guide them along their way.

Many of my best "mentors" have been the books written by Tony Robbins, Stephen R. Covey, Jim Rohn, Gary Keller, Darren Hardy, John Maxwell and David Allen.

After applying just one simple principle from one of these books, a difficult and seemingly intractable problem was solved almost overnight in my life. This drove me to fully see the power that books had to transform my life. After reading somewhere that successful people read 60 books a year on average, I immediately committed myself to reading 60 books that year. I ended up reading closer to 70 books and stretching my goal to 200 books the following year. I became obsessed with seeking knowledge and learning from others. I guess this was always built into me through my curiosity at a young age. The point is, as I became a collector of knowledge, the desire welled up inside of me to share this powerful knowledge.

Here are 10 of those profound and powerful secrets that I want to share with you now, saving you from having to read and distill the knowledge in the same way that I had to. I have incorporated many of these concepts into my Life Design Blueprint.

The 7 Habits of Highly Effective People by Stephen R. Covey

1. START WITH THE END IN MIND.

Design your lifetime goals and work backwards, as strange and perhaps counterintuitive as it may sound. Think about the end of your life, think about what you want people to say about you at your funeral, and what you wish to accomplish during your time on this beautiful planet.

Later on, I will show you how to systematically apply this in reality.

Maybe planning the end of your life doesn't seem realistic right now. Okay, let's start with one year.

Design your one-year goal, break this down into smaller monthly goals, then break those down by week. You now have a way to actually achieve this goal. There is more to this as you will see later in the book.

Think about what kind of person you need to be to reach these goals.

2. BE PROACTIVE, NOT REACTIVE.

To me, this just means take control of your life; stop reacting to outside forces and become a force that acts on outside circumstances. Many people will say this is easier said than done; however, I will show you how to make this easier to do in reality.

3. SEEK TO UNDERSTAND BEFORE YOU ASK TO BE UNDERSTOOD.

Put yourself in the other person's shoes before you expect them to understand you. This is the principle that started everything for me and transformed my life.

Failing Forward by John C. Maxwell

4. FAILURE IS GOOD AND SHOULD BE VIEWED AS A LEARNING OPPORTUNITY.

You are conditioned to fear failure through the public school system. If you get an "A," what happens to you? You are praised and rewarded by your teachers and your parents. What happens if you get an "F"? You get punished by teachers and your parents, sometimes even getting spanked for receiving a failing grade.

This basically taught you and me to be scared to try new things because you might fail at them. In my opinion, failure is actually the mother of all success.

Each and every time you fail at something, it's a lesson learned and an opportunity to use that failure to move you forward in your life. I used to say that one of my top three fears in life was not being successful, which I think is a fear shared by many other people. I now embrace failure because I realized that my most challenging, deepest and darkest times are actually my most valuable experiences in life. Without those failures, I would not be who and where I am today, and I could not be sharing this knowledge with you right now.

The Compound Effect by Darren Hardy

5. SIMPLE HABITS CAN LEAD TO MASSIVE CHANGES IN YOUR LIFE.

Here is my true story of this in action.

I quit smoking by accident. For some reason, I thought there were no cigarettes allowed on a cruise so I started using an e-cigarette. This led me to quit smoking altogether—both cigarettes and electronic ones.

I then started to make my bed every morning, which led to taking a short walk every morning before work.

Walks turned into jogs and I lost 25 pounds in 30 days.

This led me to try meditation, which changed my life forever. Just a few of the benefits:

- Calmness of mind
- No cluttered monkey mind
- No road rage
- Slow to anger
- Gratitude filled my life
- Happiness and growth in seeing major progress

This led me to read a book that transformed my life, which led me to making the commitment to read over 60 books in one year. I discovered a fire in my life for learning and growth that I now have a deep desire to share with others.

The One Thing by Gary Keller

6. YOU DON'T NEED MASSIVE DISCIPLINE TO BE SUCCESSFUL.

The super-successful people in this world do not possess superhuman discipline. They simply understand that major amounts of discipline and willpower are not what enable you to achieve the significant results you want in life. These successful individuals understand that you only need *enough* discipline to create a habit. Habits are automatic behaviors that, if leveraged in the right way, will work on autopilot to help you achieve your goals.

When you back out of your garage, your brain is acting in an automatic habitual fashion, making thousands of calculations. If you were asked to remember 100 different steps and act on them within milliseconds, your brain would probably fall out. Habits make complex behaviors automatic.

Imagine if you could program your life to automatically take you where you want to go?

You can and I'll show you how. By setting the right goals and creating the proper habits, you can achieve those goals with remarkably little effort.

For example, let's say a goal of yours is to lose 40 pounds.

By focusing on creating a few key habits, you can make losing the weight a more easily attainable goal. Some example key habits you could focus on are:

- Record your weight on a scale every day
- Do 10 to 15 minutes of exercise daily
- Drink eight glasses of water daily
- Record and mark your progress each day
- Set a target date to achieve this goal

The result may not be that you lose all 40 pounds for any number of reasons. However, you *will* make significant progress toward that goal. To my own surprise, I have often surpassed my goals using this method.

7. BE SURE TO HAVE WORTHWHILE REASONS WHY

Why do you want this goal? Your reason why is a make-it-or-break-it kind of factor.

Simply saying you want to be rich is actually a terrible goal and not very likely to become a reality for you. Research has shown that money is not a great incentive and motivator for most people. What do you want the money for? What will you do with your wealth?

8. BE VERY SPECIFIC AND INTENTIONAL ABOUT WHAT YOU WANT TO ACCOMPLISH.

Vague and broad goals are very hard to achieve. Instead of saying "I want to be happy," set a goal that you want to be living a life where you get to enjoy what you do as a _____ while traveling the world and doing _____ with the people that matter the most to you, who are _____. I want to be making $_____ per year this date and I will use this to do_____.

The Magic of Thinking Big by David J. Schwartz

9. THE BELIEF THAT YOU CAN SUCCEED CAN MAKE IT SO.

When you believe that "you can," the "how to do it" part becomes more available to you. Conversely, if you believe that you cannot do something, it almost certainly will make that true too.

A famous example is Roger Bannister in 1954 when he broke the 4-minute-mile record, which some thought was impossible. A few weeks later, someone else ran it even faster. Within a few years, many had achieved the same milestone. Today, even some high school athletes run 4-minute miles.

10. ACTION CURES FEAR, INDECISION AND PROCRASTINATION, BUT NOT TAKING ACTION WILL INCREASE FEAR AND CAUSE IT TO GROW.

By taking the first step, you remove the fear that comes with attempting something new or going after a major goal you want to accomplish. Many times, we fall into the trap of putting things off, which has been called the law of diminishing intent. The longer you wait to do something, the more likely it is you will never do it. Fear can paralyze us. I will show you how to eliminate not only the fear but also the confusion that can lead us to procrastinate. As the saying goes, a confused mind says no and does nothing. Action matched with a plan can effectively remove fear and confusion regarding what to do next.

Getting Things Done by David Allen

11. GETTING THINGS OUT OF YOUR HEAD AND ON PAPER, ALSO KNOWN AS EXTERNALIZING THOUGHTS, IS HIGHLY EFFECTIVE.

Large, complex and often challenging projects can be made exponentially easier by putting them on paper rather than working things out solely in your mind.

Our mind handles things that live outside of our minds far better than it handles internal thoughts, so putting your thoughts in a physical form will help you to more effectively solve complex problems. For example, starting a new business is a massively complex challenge to figure out entirely in your mind. You may think about the different types of businesses you could start. What would you sell or offer? How much would you charge? How would you market your offering? Who will create what you offer? Who will design your website? Who do you know that does websites? Will you need employees? Do you need a lawyer? What about tax structure? The list could go on and on and, by this time, your brain will probably hurt or you will have given up on the idea altogether. If you simply took out a piece of paper and started to write out all these different questions, you could easily and quickly begin to map out all these issues in a way that would make much more sense, and your mind would be better able to figure out these challenges. In my opinion, this is one of the main reasons that the Life Design Blueprint is so effective. It externalizes many potential task and challenges that are colliding in our minds and fighting for attention. Throw in the added stress of unexpected surprises we have to adapt to, and it's no wonder that people say, "I'm so tired I don't even want to think." Bringing clarity to complex projects is easy when you externalize your thoughts and ideas. Think of your mind like a computer's memory—you only have so much short-term memory to use at one time.

12. THE ABILITY TO ENVISION SUCCESS—EVEN WHEN THE PATH TO ACHIEVING IT IS NOT CLEAR AT ALL—IS NOT HOCUS-POCUS, POSITIVE-THINKING BULLSHIT. IT HAS SCIENTIFIC ROOTS.

It's called the reticular activating system (RAS) in the brain, and it acts like your very own Google search engine. When you define what you want a desired outcome to be, your RAS will filter items that match the vision you have already defined. A common example of this is found in the *Personal MBA* by Josh Kaufman, in which he calls to our attention that when you decide that you want a certain kind of car, it causes you to see this type of car everywhere. That car did not, all of a sudden, become more popular. Your brain now calls it to your attention when previously it was filtered out. The method for doing something is revealed once you envision the desired outcome, because your brain will find the path forward that you may have been previously overlooking.

This idea is fascinating to me. There is detailed research that supports this. World-class peak performers and Olympic athletes use a form of visualization where they imagine the successful outcome in detail. They literally imagine themselves crossing the finish line before everyone else. This allows them to actually perform at higher levels. Using this visualization method can bring about significant improvements.

For more information on the RAS system, I recommend *The Ultimate Edge* by Tina Thomas, Phd.

13. KNOWING WHAT THE NEXT ACTION IS WILL CREATE CLARITY AND MOVE YOU TOWARD YOUR DESIRED OUTCOMES.

When you define your stated purpose for a specific goal, there are many related benefits. It not only defines success, but it also gives you the criteria for making decisions. This will help you to align your resources. It motivates, clarifies and helps you to focus your attention. Once you define the purpose behind your desire to complete this goal, deciding on your subsequent actions will be much easier. By knowing what your very next action will be, you are able to take action and avoid the confusion, procrastination and frustration often associated with not knowing the entire answer to how you will accomplish the larger task as a whole. This is a simplified explanation, but it is a key concept that contributes to the effectiveness of the Life Design Blueprint.

4

The Three Creations

Nothing is created only once. There are three creations for virtually everything that exists in our reality.

The three creations are:

1. In the mind
2. On paper or digitally
3. In reality

This may seem like common sense to some while it may escape others entirely. Let's look at some examples. Think about when a home is being built. The house must first be imagined in the mind of the architect, home builder or the prospective home owner.

Then detailed plans are used to create blueprints and schematics, lists of required materials and so forth. This would be the second time that this home is being created. After this, and only after this, can a home be actually built. Contractors build the house according to those detailed specifications and blueprints. What do you think would happen if the contractors attempted to build the house without any kind of blueprint? I would argue three points.

1. The home could not be built effectively.

2. There would be massive amounts of wasted time, effort, energy and money.

3. You may not end up with exactly the house you wanted.

Think about how many people have tried putting together IKEA furniture without instructions. How many times did you curse the simple desk you couldn't keep together because you had seven leftover screws? And then you decided to look at the instructions.

As another example, let's briefly explore the history of the toilet. Humans used to dig holes in the dirt and do their business in holes. Some people still do this today and it works out in the wilderness. Then came the dry-earth closet also known as the composting toilet. This is your outhouse-style toilet. Then there was something called the "flying toilet" in Tanzania. People used to do the deed in a type of bag and then fling it as far as they could. Imagine trying to dodge flying bags of human shit? The practice got banned for obvious reasons. Then, at some point, along came the flushing toilet. What does the history of toilets have to do with my Life Design Blueprint? Let's examine the chronicles of the toilet further.

- People would get sick from improperly discarded human waste.
- Someone imagined a new kind of toilet.
- Eventually, someone drew up plans.
- Then the physical flushing toilet was created.
- We found a better way to get rid of waste.

The toilet was also created three times.
The three creations:

- In the mind
- On paper
- In real life

Your goals must also go through these stages. It's not enough to imagine or dream of a better life. You must design and plan your life meticulously; then you can easily go and create the life that you designed.

Here are the steps broken down in a simple way:

Imagine: Think of the life you want. Use your imagination and don't be afraid to dream big.

Develop a plan: You must create a detailed and meticulous plan.

Create: Go and take action on the plan you created to make those goals a reality.

Measure: Track and measure your results and progress.

Review and revise: Through the tracking and measuring of your progress, you can see what works and what does not work and make adjustments. The key to this step is the frequent review process.

An acronym I came up with to help me remember these steps is **IDCMR,** which stands for "Imagine, Develop, Create, Measure, Review. If you wanted a sentence to remember here's one "I didn't create my reality" because, if you don't use these steps, it's my opinion that you won't be able to create the reality you want. If you do not follow these steps, I strongly believe that you will have to expend significantly more resources in terms of time, effort, energy and money in order to reach your goals.

Does all this sound exhausting yet? Does the word *meticulous* remind you of the pain you feel when walking into a tiny DMV office with a broken AC system that is crowded with 300 sweaty people? For a long time, the very idea of detailed and meticulous planning made me cringe.

I considered myself more of a go-with-the-flow kind of person, and I valued my ability to be spontaneous and make changes and choices in my life as needed.

Then I discovered that *systems create freedom.*

No bullshit! Systems, structure and planning create and give you more *freedom.*

My mind was blown when I discovered this. I will demonstrate this further throughout the book. For now, just remember that if you want more freedom, then you need to have externalized systems for accomplishing tasks.

5

Why Use a Blueprint?

By creating and using a Life Design Blueprint, you will be able to put your goals on autopilot. By focusing your limited willpower on establishing the right habits, you can fulfill those goals through virtually automatic behavior. You will be able to make major progress on the goals you set for your life and achieve the goals you have always dreamed about.

Using a blueprint will give you a sense of excitement about your life and what you are doing for several reasons. First, you'll be able identify where you are now and chart a course to where you want to be. If you have ever tried going somewhere you have never been before without GPS or a map, you may have gotten lost along the way. By using the blueprint, you will see measurable progress, and I believe that one of the keys to happiness is making true progress in your life.

You will develop an almost mystical power against procrastination and will be able to stick to your commitments—most importantly, the commitments you make to yourself. I can't tell you how sad it makes me feel when I see all the cynical social media posts around New Year's Eve, about how everyone should quit all the "new year, new me bull-shit." This blueprint will help you turn those resolutions into reality. If you decide to use a blueprint to design your life, you will always know the very next thing you need to do to move closer to your goals. You will lose the confusion and frustration that comes with not knowing what to do next or how to go about it.

You will be able to find more purpose and clarity in your life and feel a deep sense of happiness because you are moving forward and you know where you are going. These are just some of the many benefits I found though my own Life Design Blueprint. This sounds complicated, but I will break it down for you soon.

But first, let me tell you a quick short personal story. I set my goals for the next year during the last few months of the current year. I found myself at the end of 2016 having made some great progress in my life over the year, but I was hungry and I wanted more, so I took the time to map out what I wanted for 2017. I broke things down and put it all on paper externally. This process morphed into my very first prototype of the Life Design Blueprint.

I was able to create my Life Design Blueprint in less than one weekend. Remember the term *return on investment*? This was one of the best investments I could have ever made. Setting my goals the year before was nothing new for me. To get started, I followed a few simple steps:

- Took a trip to Office Depot (you could be lazy and order everything you need on Amazon today)
- Bought a printer, ink and paper
- Embraced my overwhelming desire to make 2017 my best year yet

Within the first 30 days of the year, I reached goals that I anticipated would take me months. It transformed my life, and I immediately felt a deep desire to share this with as many people as I possibly could.

I felt happiness and witnessed major progress toward my goals in life.

I felt gratitude and excitement each day in waking up and thinking about how I could improve myself.

I deeply and sincerely hope my Life Design Blueprint helps you as much as it has helped me. My life is filled with massive dreams that I now feel I am actually on the path toward achieving—because I created a method and system that works for me.

PROFOUND WORDS CAN INSPIRE US TO ACT!

Here are some quotes that really impacted me that also relate to the concepts behind the Life Design Blueprint.

"People do not decide their futures, they decide their habits and their habits decide their future."

—FM Alexander

"We are what we repeatedly do. Excellence, then is not an act, but a habit."

—Aristotle

"Your net worth to the world is usually determined by what remains after your bad habits are subtracted from your good ones."

—Benjamin Franklin

"Successful people are simply those with successful habits."

—Brian Tracy

Do you see a recurring theme here? I wholeheartedly believe that habits determine the outcome of your life.

PUT YOUR GOALS ON AUTOPILOT

The most surefire way to do this is to ensure that your *habits* are leading you to automatically fulfill your goals. Bad habits *do not* take super human willpower to break. Here are the two tips that gave me power over all my habits.

To break a habit, don't try to stop it; just replace it with a better one.

Willpower runs out; however, you only need enough willpower to make a new habit. You see, habits once formed will do the rest of the hard work.

Remember the calculations we spoke about earlier when you're trying to back out of your garage. Do you honestly think that you remember every single calculation or do you think your brain is just following a habitual routine? We can do this with our goals.

MAKE MAJOR PROGRESS AND BUILD MOMENTUM

Tracking your victories and failures on a weekly basis will create momentum as you can physically see the progress you are making.

Barely three weeks into the new year, I had made major progress on several major goals that should have taken me longer.

- I broke into a very hard-to-reach industry while skipping some steps thought to be required.
- I lost a quarter of my weight loss goal.
- I discovered my most powerful new weapon in achieving the results I wanted for my life.
- I developed different ways to create passive income.
- I created my first ebook and audiobook.
- I grew my professional network massively.

- I landed a consulting contract.
- I devoured 12 books, retained much of the knowledge and put it all into action.
- The first month of the year wasn't even over yet.

I'm not sharing this with you to impress you but to impress upon you the power that I believe is derived from creation of my own Life Design Blueprint.

FEEL EXCITEMENT AND KNOW WHERE YOU ARE GOING!

Identify where you are and chart a path taking you to where you want to be. When you make measurable progress, it creates excitement and purpose in your life. You will feel ready to wake up and be energized to make more progress. A side effect of this is that you will gain power and confidence over your life by being the deliberate designer of it. By starting with the end-game result in mind and working things out backwards, you will have a confidence you may have never felt before. I will go into more detail later on in the book about how we can specifically accomplish this. Through all of this, I have discovered a greater sense of happiness in my life.

PRO-CRAS-TI-NA-TION

As a lifelong creative type, I have struggled with habitual $%&#^@*&^@%#&^! Beeeeep! Yes, it's a bad word to me. I can now manage, block out my time and efforts and actually get things *done*!

> "Not managing your time and making excuses are two bad habits. Don't put them both together by claiming you don't have the time."
>
> —Bo Bennett

This quote was like a kick in the stomach when I first saw it. How many times did I say, "Oh, I don't have the time to do all that"? I have learned the more effort you put into planning something out, generally the faster and smoother the process will go.

STICK TO YOUR WORD AND COMMITMENTS

Promises to yourself are the most important ones to keep. We have all made commitments, resolutions and promises only to break those promises. My Life Design Blueprint has helped me to remain committed to my most important promises to myself and I hope it can do the same for you. No longer do I feel the guilt of making promises to myself that I don't keep.

CLEARLY SEE WHERE YOU WANT TO GO, MAKE DAILY PROGRESS AND REVIEW YOUR ACTIONS.

The process of reviewing your progress and results allows you to make corrections quickly. You will also make observations that will create incredible clarity of purpose and direction. You will no longer get stuck thinking about what to do next. This improved clarity has made a massive difference for me!

The Life Design Blueprint Formula™

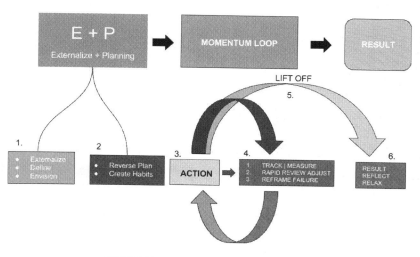

E + P
Externalize + Planning

MOMENTUM LOOP

RESULT

LIFT OFF
5.

1.
- Externalize
- Define
- Envision

2
- Reverse Plan
- Create Habits

3.
ACTION

4.
1. TRACK | MEASURE
2. RAPID REVIEW ADJUST
3. REFRAME FAILURE

6.
RESULT
REFLECT
RELAX

3 PART FORMULA of YOUR LIFE DESIGN BLUEPRINT
6 STAGES OF PROGRESSION
12 STEP PROCESS
By ALBERT POLANCO

Here Is the Formula Simplified on the next page

Externalized Planning + Momentum Loop + Liftoff = Result

Let's take a moment to break this down.

EXTERNALIZED PLANNING DEFINED

Formula Breakdown: **EDEN = Externalize + Define + Envision**
Externalize: **Verb**
Definition: Give external existence or form to.
Project (a mental image or process) onto a figure outside oneself.

WHAT NEEDS TO BE EXTERNALIZED?

- **Where you are right now in your life.**
  - You can't chart a path to a destination without knowing the starting point first.
- **Your past narrative.**
  - What has happened in your life during the last few years that has lead you to this point.
- **Your limiting BS (belief systems)**
  - I'm not good at that.
  - I have a full-time job; I can't start a business.
  - I'm just big boned; I can't lose weight.
  - I'm no good at money.
  - Rich people are evil and wasteful.
  - I'll never be able to do that.
  - I don't have the time.
  - I'm not smart enough to do that.
  - I don't know how to do that.
  - I'm not worth enough to earn that much money.

1 Externalized Goals

Moving your goals from your mind onto paper in physical form is called externalization, and this upgrades your "wish" into what you can now actually call a goal. If you do not take the time to write out your goals, then you will almost certainly not achieve them. I totally understand that you may feel resistance to writing down a goal that you don't know how to accomplish or even believe you can achieve at the moment. Don't let that inner voice hold you back. The *how* is not important; the *what* and *why* are most important. This is normal. Everyone who achieves anything has this same negative inner voice. It's part of our physical brain that was supposed to protect us back during caveman times. Now it works against us sometimes. Later in this book, you will learn more about how to silence and overcome this inner voice. I would like to share a strong opinion that I know will ruffle many feathers out there.

SMART GOALS ARE BULLSH^T!

Yes, I'm saying that specific, measurable, agreed-upon, realistic and time-based goals are a novel idea; yet I find this framework to be incomplete.

2 MAJOR PROBLEMS WITH SMART GOALS

I hate the word "**realistic.**" **WTF is that?**

- People have made millions of dollars in a just a few days, yet few people would see that as a realistic goal.
- Breakthrough discoveries can happen from one day to the next that were not realistic the day before.

- Major breakthroughs happen in people's lives in *seconds* that were never considered realistic.

To me, "realistic" means "Yeah, I can go to the store and pick up a gallon of milk, provided my car or legs will take me there, without getting hit by a car or getting into an accident on the way there and back. I should realistically be able to get there and bring home some milk."

THE UNREALISTIC PLANET WE LIVE ON

Trillions of systems and processes and forces in our universe combined together at just the right time in just the right way, down to the most infinitely perfect detail, to make life on earth possible? This is supposed to all be some realistic coincidence?

If we were just a little farther from the sun, we would freeze and billions of lifeforms on our beautiful planet would have never existed.

If we were just a little bit closer to the sun, our climate would have been dramatically different and life as we know it would not have been "realistic or possible."

THE HUMAN BODY

The human body is a miraculous combination of perfect systems that all work together to keep us alive and healthy when maintained and given the proper fuel. Let's not even get into the infinitely complex system that makes up our brains. These things, to the majority of human beings, are not understood fully or considered to be realistic.

Hate is a such a strong word, but I do *hate* the word "realistic," especially when talking about goals. I do not believe that we have the right to squander this amazingly precious opportunity we have to be alive in order to aim for what one considers to be realistic.

BE LIKE ELON

Inspiring human beings like Elon Musk would never have been possible if he had made only realistic goals. His company's stated mission, according to Tesla.com, is to accelerate the world's transition to sustainable energy.

Before Elon Musk, was that realistic for the traditional automotive manufacturers? I'll go ahead and say, "*hell no!*" Do you know why? Because all the other manufacturers set "realistic goals" in order to continue business as usual.

Elon Musk was also a co-founder of the solar power company SolarCity. Lyndon and Peter Rive have created the most recognized clean energy company on the planet.

It was *unrealistic* to think that solar energy would ever be cheaper to produce than traditional fossil fuels. According to the SolarCity website: "We make clean energy available to homeowners, businesses, schools, non-profits and government organizations at a lower cost than they pay for energy generated by burning fossil fuels like coal, oil and natural gas."

In 2001, Musk founded SpaceX, a spacecraft design and manufacturing company that has both advanced the technology to unprecedented levels and inspired a new space race among the world's most recognized titans of industry, while at the same time lowering the costs astronomically. The company has competed with and overtaken national governments from all over the world who were the *only* ones previously able to explore space in any meaningful way.

Was this realistic? Musk came from a humble background as a South African immigrant. He founded PayPal and eventually taught himself how to be a rocket scientist from reading books.

His stated goal for SpaceX from its inception has been to revolutionize space technology in order to protect all of humankind from extinction by making human life multi-planetary, with our first colony on Mars. He plans to eventually terraform and create a livable atmosphere on Mars using thermonuclear devices to kickstart the planet. We're talking about taking a *whole freaking* planet that is not livable for us at the moment and transforming it to be able to sustain human life one day. Does this sound realistic to you right now?

People used to laugh at Elon Musk when he stated he would do something that would change the world. Now he tweets companies into existence.

Elon Musk is also involved in:

- Artificial intelligence
- A revolutionary high-speed transportation system known as the hyperloop
- A vertical takeoff and landing supersonic jet air-craft that is powered by an *electric* motor known as the Musk Electric Jet
- The Boring Company, which will relieve LA traffic by boring tunnels underground

DOES ANY OF THAT SOUND REALISTIC TO YOU?

Elon Musk never listened to what anyone considered to be realistic. In fact, what is realistic and what is thought to be realistic are often very different things. I fully believe that I will be able to travel to Mars in my lifetime and dock at a space station named after Musk himself. The entire human race could survive a possible extinction event because of the impact he has had on our world. This one person has had the courage to dream for our entire species. If that's not unrealistic yet inspiring at the same time, then I don't know what is. Okay, I'm done. We can now get off the Musk train. Thank you for riding.

I wanted to emphasize why realistic is the wrong word to use when setting any kind of goal. It is not inspiring to set the goal of: "I want to pay my bills on time and have a few hundred dollars left over at the end of the month. So after a year of working 40+ hours a week, I get the privilege of begging my boss to let me take two weeks off." This is so uninspiring and actually sets us up to live smaller lives, much smaller than we were ever intended to live.

The phrase we should be using is "believable to you." Because what is realistic for you is going to be based on you and your internal mental limitations. You can actually do anything you want. It is only your mental internal limitations that will stop you from achieving. You must believe in the possibility for you, even if you have no clue how to get there. When you believe that it's possible, the *how* will present itself if you follow the proper steps I'm going to share in this book.

THE 2ND REASON WHY SMART GOALS ARE BULLSH*&!

They may sound wonderful in theory, but they are missing a key and, in my opinion, the most critical aspect of providing a good framework for setting a goal, which is a process or system to attain this well-defined goal you want to achieve.

GOALS ARE JUST RESULTS WE WANT

I have consolidated and compiled a new framework that can be used to not only set and define your goals but also to put achieving your goals on autopilot with a step-by-step system and process.

I want to be clear on a few things ahead of time. No idea or creation is actually completely original in and of itself. Everything that is ever created is made up of parts from various sources. Even if you think that you created something, you did not. It came from something else that you have been exposed to. This is as true for Albert Einstein as it was for Leonardo da Vinci. Everything we create is based on parts and pieces of other created things.

COMPRESSING TIME AND LEARNING FASTER THROUGH OTHERS

At the time of writing this book, I have read and digested just shy of 100 books in the last year and a few months. All of my reading was personal development and improvement related. I have absorbed a massive amount of information from some of the most brilliant minds on our planet, not counting the thousands of dollars I have invested in improving my skills through video training and online courses.

I say all this not to brag but to make my next point, which is that my system has been developed from combining, curating and experimenting with systems and methods learned from hundreds of different sources. I found a formula that not only has worked miracles for myself, but that I believe wholeheartedly can be applied to the lives of others to make meaningful changes.

Today's masters and gurus were mentored by and learned from the most brilliant minds—some reading hundreds and thousands of books to gain the knowledge and insight that they now possess.

#2 Define and Decide on Your Goals

- The Tony Robbins Method of goal setting is a piece of the puzzle.
- What goals?
- In what areas of your life?
- Why these goals and not others?
- Specifically, why do you want them?

I break his method down in detail later on in this book. I just wanted to give you an overview for right now.

Once we have our list of goals that are meaningful, with truly inspiring reasons why we need to attain them, then we need to refine and narrow them down further.

MOST IMPORTANT GOAL SHOWDOWN

As the saying goes, you can do anything you want in this world; you just can't do everything you want. Limiting the number and theme of our goals during certain periods of time is critical to this process and framework. So, we will use the Tony Robbins Method to develop inspiring and worthwhile goals; then we will apply some limits and refine them further. You may have come up with several goals in various areas of your life. We need to simplify and group goals together. We will face the goals off against each other in a showdown that, once finished, will provide you with a much more concise and tightly relatable set of goals. This step is critical for your success. You should be forming a common theme for these goals for your first 90-day cycle.

JUST ON THE HORIZON IS 90 DAYS

It is important to have a long-term vision for our lives extending out into one-year, three-year and five-year goals. However, let's not call those goals anymore for the purpose of understanding this process and framework. We will simplify and break things down into four quarters or 90-day cycles. We are setting goals for the next 90 days, which does not mean you cannot have one-year goals; it just means those one-year goals will be broken down and mapped out into 90-day cycles. This will immediately make the goal more believable and attainable to you. The 90-day period makes sense because it's enough time to accomplish something significant, yet it's not an overwhelmingly long time. You'll see encouraging results fairly quickly.

It is my belief that with this system of setting 90-day goals, correctly formed and executed, you can outperform your entire last year in just 90 days. Imagine having the ability to advance at least three years' worth of your most meaningful and impactful goals in the span of only one year. That's the power of this way of setting and attaining goals.

THE STANDARD PACE IS FOR CHUMPS

I came up with the concept for this book, did all the prewriting, outlining, editing, revising, publishing and marketing in less than 90 days while still completing some of the other 90 day goals I've been working on. The common time frame I found everywhere for writing and publishing a book was one full year at minimum. I love the quote that I heard from CD Baby founder Derek Sivers. One of his teachers told him, "The standard pace is for chumps." I agree. If I can get the results others take a year to get, inside of 90 days, I will continue to press on at this pace for as long as I desire to. I do have to build in periods of reflection and relaxation as well.

#3 Envision

To recap, the first part of the formula was:

1. Externalize
2. Decide and define
3. Envision

You must be able to envision and visualize the goal you want to attain; it needs to be something you can imagine and feel in your mind. This is how the top world-class athletes are able to perform at such high levels. There have been athletes who have been brain-scanned during their practice of mentally envisioning a task, and brain scans show the same level of activity as if the athlete were physically completing the task.

REMEMBER TO ENVISION YOUR GOAL

- See your desired outcome
- You do not need to know the *how* yet
- Believe in the possibility
- Less than 90 days away

If you can see and feel yourself living in the desired outcome, this will program your brain and subconscious to do what it does best: recognize patterns. This pattern recognition will help you to discover the *how* even if previously you had no idea how on earth you would achieve the intended goal.

The Next Step Is the REVERSE PLAN

Remember, start with the outcome in mind. Express in writing what would need to happen for that goal to come to fruition in the next 90 days. Break it down into steps with major milestones guiding the way. These steps and milestones need to be easily measurable numbers.

For example, if you want to increase your income over the next 90 days, you would need to set strategic performance indicators that are specific and measurable with a date attached. These are the numbers that you need along the way to reaching your 90-day goal. Remember, it needs to be tangible and measurable. Stating "I want to make more money in the next 90 days" is not specific enough.

For example, this is a properly written outcome goal or result.

I will improve my income from $5,000 a month to $8,000 per month by March 21, 2017 (90 days away).

We then break that milestone goal down into two-week segments, and it becomes easier. Here is the math to simplify things for you. In a 90-day period, there will be roughly 6.4 periods that are 14 days long each.

Let's use these same numbers for this example.

I want to increase my income by $3,000 over the next 90 days ($8,000 to $5,000 = $3,000)

That breaks down to $1,000 per 30 days, an increase of $500 every two weeks.

3-STEP REVERSE PLAN PROCESS TO MAKE THIS HAPPEN

1. Define the result
2. Define the performance milestone (strategic performance indicator)
   - I will improve _____ from this number to this number by this date (two weeks away)
3. Define the tasks and processes that need to happen to meet the above milestone

This is where things get really powerful!

Define the process and tasks attached to your performance milestone.

The criteria you need to define for a task or process to be specific enough is:

- Who is doing the task?
- What is the task or process?
- When will this task be taking place?
- Why is this task being completed?
- How will it move you forward?

Remember, these tasks need to be tied to and moving toward the milestones you set above.

Here is an example of this in action.

Each Friday, I will spend two hours in the afternoon working on creating my social media posts for the next two weeks. This is being completed by me to give to my designer in order to increase the incoming leads for my business. I will save this as a Google document in my Google drive under the social media folder.

On Friday, March 29, I will create a list of 14 quotes that I want my graphic designer Joel to turn into Instagram marketing images we can post once per day for the next two weeks. This will increase our brand's engagement online and generate more leads for my business.

OVERKILL?

You might be saying, wow, that's super detailed. Isn't that a little over-kill? Nope. The more specific you are, the more clarity and momentum you will create around this task. Believe me, the first time I did this, it was hard. But when I was done, I had literally every single task I needed to complete for the next two weeks mapped out and scheduled in my Google calendar. The most incredible sense of freedom came from knowing I would not be missing anything that was critically important to moving my life forward toward my goals. I got more done in one day after using this method than I had been able to accomplish during the previous five days combined.

I actually restructured and revised and rewrote major parts of the book you're reading now after just one day of using this method. I had the most productive day I had ever experienced and, since that day, my level of get-shit-done has increased exponentially.

In the Life Design Blueprint Workbook, there is a section that will help you to master this process.

I want to take this opportunity to write another curse word in my book.

FU^% MULTITASKING

Researchers at the University of Sussex found that multitasking can lead to a permanent drop in IQ. There was a loss in brain density when measured by an MRI machine.

There have been numerous studies on the negative effects of multitasking, which include the following:

- Losing 40% of your productivity
- Lowers your IQ up to 10 points
- Makes any task take much longer
- Takes an average of 23 minutes to get back on task

NO ONE CAN ACTUALLY MULTITASK

It is a myth. When you attempt to multitask, your brain is actually switching between task 1 and task 2 each and every time, which causes something called the cognitive switching penalty. You actually use more energy and get less done when switching between tasks. This is why you can be busy all day long at work or at home doing all the various tasks you need to do, feel worn out, yet still accomplish very little.

This mental penalty just causes stress in our lives. Losing nearly half of your time because you think you can multitask is not helping you in any way.

This is a major reason so many people say there is just too much to get done in a day and not enough time to do it. If you have said this, chances are you do an enormous amount of cognitive switching in your day.

HERE ARE SOME NUMBERS

1 project	100% of available time	0 loss to switching
2 projects at once	40% of available time	20% loss to switching
3 projects at once	20% of available time	40% loss to switching
4 projects at once	10% of available time	

With four hours of multitasking, you lose 40% of the available time, which is equal to 96 minutes out of 240 minutes. That is an incredible loss, all because you're trying to do more than one thing at a time.

INTERRUPTIONS COUNT AS SWITCHING

We have all been there, trying to get something important done sitting at the desk in the home office. Then all of a sudden, your phone dings and it's got your attention. As you reach for your phone, an important email comes into your inbox, so you put your phone down to try and read the email. As you look up to read the email, you look back down to see if you can read a text really fast in the notification bar without unlocking your phone. A few words in the text catch your eye, so now you are back to looking at your phone. It's a funny video your friend is telling you to watch. So, you watch it halfway through. You didn't find it funny, so you open up your Facebook tab and, right smack dab in the middle, someone posted a political post that pisses you off. You start to think about how you're going to make them feel stupid with your clever response in the comment box. They message back, leaving a new comment that makes you even angrier than the original post, calling you a liberal Republican, Nazi hippie, Barack Obama loving Donald Trump supporting anarchist. You're now fuming and can't remember why you even got on Facebook. You were supposed to be working on that important project before you got interrupted. It's two hours later and you have no idea what has happened to the time and have nothing to show for it.

This happens almost every day to many people.

THE ANSWER TO THIS PROBLEM IS TWO-FOLD.

Time Management is MORE BULL&^&%!

- You cannot manage time. It literally will pass the same way if you have a full calendar or not.
- Time is not—in any way, shape or form—something you can manage.

COMMON SENSE IS SOMETIMES WRAPPED IN STUPID

This is one of those universal sayings that people hear so often they never even bother to think about how it is that a person can manage time if it stops for no one.

Can you call a timeout and ask time to stop and wait for you to catch up on the Instagram post you were looking at? Can you ask time to slow down and speed up? Can you pay time more money so that it will work for you longer?

NO! Time management is not possible.

You need TASK MANAGEMENT. You need to manage the activities you are doing as time passes.

Time is just a container. You choose what you put in that container.

There always seems to be something we have to respond to in our daily lives. You are at work and three people at three different times within 10 minutes enter your office to ask you about something they need help with. Then your supervisor sends you an email asking you to confirm that you read the three-line email for a meeting that's happening in two weeks. The phone rings and it's a client who then puts you on hold. I'm sure this is starting to sound like your reality. In fact, you're not alone. This is how many people's work lives are structured.

We are always reacting to the outside world, and if the world would just stop for a second so we could have a minute to get our SHI*& together, we could actually get something done, right?

Remember the habit "Be proactive" from the *7 Habits of Highly Effective People*. We are going to take a page from that book called the Eisenhower matrix.

Here is what it looks like.

The final step in this first part of a 3-part formula is to create habits.

This is actually the part of the process that I believe sets the best goal-setting systems apart. The idea that we must rely on sheer will-power and hard work to achieve our goals is missing, in my opinion, the most powerful human driver or behavior. Our habits are automatic routines our brains follow in order to save us time, energy and effort. Your brain is only a tiny percentage of your entire body, yet it consumes up to 25% of your energy. That's a lot of energy, so in order to be more efficient and conserve energy, our brains like to follow automatic patterns of behavior that require little energy to accomplish. Have you ever been driving down a long stretch of road on a road trip and noticed that you had 200 miles to your destination; then in what felt like only a few short minutes later, you saw another sign saying 120 miles to your destination? You think, wait a minute, how the hell did I get so far so fast? You can't remember the last 80 miles or the hour that has passed.

The truth is that you sort of checked out mentally and relied on your automatic habit routines of driving and staying inside of the lines on the road. It's always smart to remain alert while on the road; however, I know I have been there, and it happens to all of us at some point.

The point I am making is that you can use these automatic behaviors to actually propel you forward toward your goals if you learn how to program the habits that will take you where you want to go. This is truly like putting your goals on autopilot as you will be using much less effort and energy in order to accomplish the things that you want in life. This is what the Life Design Blueprint is all about.

I will go over in much more detail how to create and form the correct habits later on in this book. For now, I just want to give you an overall picture of what this entire process looks like.

The Momentum Loop

After creating habits, we move into what I call the Momentum Loop. This part has five key steps that combine to form the Momentum Loop.

1. Action
2. Track & Measure Progress
3. Rapid Review & Adjust
4. Reframe Failure & Stack Wins
5. Liftoff

Let's examine each in order.

ACTION

Because you did the previous steps discussed earlier, you set the right goals, and you defined the reasons why they were important to you. You envisioned your outcome and result. You planned from the end result backwards and you selected the right habits to form. Now you are ready to take action on your plan. This part is easy once you do the initial hard work, which I call frontloading your life's goals. As with any complex project with many moving parts, the more you take the right amount of time to map out and set a properly defined plan of action, the faster and easier it will be to take specific actions. This is where you'll find that this system gives you more freedom. Because if you did the first parts right, you will have a highly detailed plan of action to follow. You no longer have to expend massive amounts of mental energy trying to figure out what you need to be doing now or what comes next. You will also now have the ability, in the action phase, to see if your plan will be feasible and what it actually takes in reality to accomplish it. Don't worry. You are sure to overestimate and underestimate certain aspects. This is all okay. Just take action and move into the next phase of this Momentum Loop.

TRACK AND MEASURE PROGRESS

By using a visual form of tracking daily progress on your habits and activities related to your goals, you will see measurable progress through your weeks, and this creates a feeling of excitement and momentum, knowing and seeing that you are moving toward your goals daily. This step is critical to the entire overall 12-step process because without the tracking and measuring of your progress, it becomes very hard to track your progress mentally. We often will forget how many things we got right and how far we have come after just facing one difficult situation. This is just how our brains are wired. By tracking and measuring your progress, you will feel increased motivation, momentum and excitement every day, and this increase will keep compounding into more and more momentum and energy propelling you toward your goal.

RAPID REVIEW AND ADJUST

Each step in this process builds upon the last in an interconnected way. This step is all about course correction and making sure you learn and adjust from each week's progress. Some of your best observations will happen during this review time. By taking 45 minutes to one hour one day a week to review your progress for the week, it will keep you moving on the right track. You will see what is working for you and what is not working for you, so that you can plan accordingly for the next week. My review day is Sunday evenings and it is scheduled in my Google calendar every Sunday at 9pm to 10:30pm from now until *forever*. This time is absolutely sacred to me and has been incredibly valuable to me in my own journey.

REFRAME FAILURE AND STACK YOUR WINS

This step is a part of my weekly review. However, it is so important that it requires its own step here. We have been trained since we were little children to fear failure, and most of us will avoid talking about or even thinking about our failures. This is normal human nature. Failing is uncomfortable and makes us feel defeated. I know. I have been there more times than I can count. Failing at something you have devoted tons of effort to can be soul crushing and devastating, until you learn how to reframe your failures to be your friend. Because of our programming from a public education system and a society that have taught us failure is something bad, we do not know how to effectively deal with failure. Failure is one of the most valuable things we can do. The faster we can fail and learn from those failures, the faster we will be moving in a more intelligent direction. This step is about writing out what didn't work and being really brutally honest about why you failed at this particular thing. Write it down. Don't just think about it. Often, what we think and what we see in writing will be drastically different.

Here are the steps of this process:

1. Write down what did not work and what you failed at.

2. Write out why you honestly believe that you failed at this.

3. Write out 3–5 ways you can improve those things.

4. Write out how you will implement those things to improve and turn this into a success.

This process could be very simple or very elaborate. It's up to you. You just need to make sure that you do this. When you externalize the failure and you see it in writing and you see in writing why it did not work, you can start to identify patterns that you would have never seen in your head.

Stack up all your wins from the week and write them out somewhere you can see. This shows you really how far you've come and how much progress you are making. Even when you occasionally stumble, it gives you a sense of perspective to lean on. Our brains are negativity magnets because we evolved that way as a survival mechanism. Our caveman brains do not serve us well today in this aspect. We overemphasize the negative things and gloss over the positives. Our media, society and people around us reinforce this negative alertness tendency. Think about what you hear on the news day in and day out. The saying used to be that good news doesn't sell newspapers. This unfortunately is true for other types of news media as well. People who remove the news from their lives actually feel more enjoyment, calmness and trust toward people. The benefits are enormous. I myself avoid 99.9% of all news media, newspapers, news sites. This has improved my life, mood, energy and trust level with other human beings, so I choose to keep it this way.

WE HAVE LIFTOFF!

The last part of what I call the Momentum Loop is liftoff. Every week, you will take action, measure progress, review and make adjustments, and this process forms a loop. Once you start making progress and building momentum going through this loop week by week, you will reach the point where you will be launched out of the loop and flying straight toward your result. Your mood and energy will be at peak levels during this liftoff phase as you can see the result closer on the horizon and you can see a clear path to this result that you planned. This stage is one of the most exciting parts of this entire process. To give you a visual image, imagine racing those electronic toy race cars on tracks you put together by hand. What happens when you go too fast on the track around a corner? Your car flies off the track, some may call this a crash for our purposes let's say your car has a rocket engine that can only be used when it flies off the track. This is precisely what happens to you as your life moves toward your goals.

You are working on forming your habits, tracking progress, making adjustments and, all of a sudden, this momentum force becomes so strong that you find yourself flying toward your goal. Look at it below in this diagram.

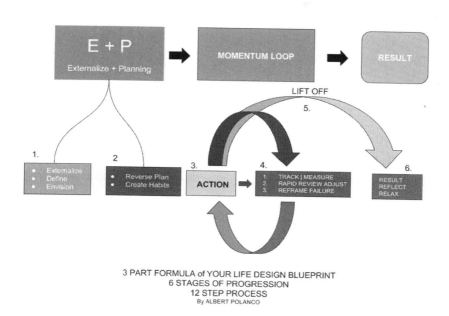

3 PART FORMULA of YOUR LIFE DESIGN BLUEPRINT
6 STAGES OF PROGRESSION
12 STEP PROCESS
By ALBERT POLANCO

The third and final part of the 3-part formula is your RESULT.

YOUR RESULT AND OUTCOME REALIZED

You made it. You arrived at your 90-day goal. It's time to enjoy and celebrate this major win in your life. This was made up of smaller wins, losses, reviews and adjustments, but you're here. You made it. So what's next? What comes next is the final step, which is to reflect and relax.

REFLECT AND RELAX

Reflect on the entire process over the last 90 days. Now you have the ability to look over your notes for the last 90 days and see all the valuable lessons you learned, all the little wins adding up over time to create this major win for you. It's important to take a while to relax at this stage and spend a day doing something special in celebration of a job well done. If this goal is only a part of your larger one-year goal, then get yourself ready to start a new cycle, this time with even more momentum, confidence and knowledge about how you will be able to get everything you want in life using the Life Design Blueprint Formula.

This is a highly summarized bird's-eye view of the entire Life Design Blueprint Formula. I will dive deeper into the *how* and give you the tools you need in order to actually make all this happen. Let's move on into further exploring the Life Design Blueprint.

7

What Is It and How Do I Create One?

Here are the basic materials you need to create your own Life Design Blueprint.

- 2-inch 3-ring binder
- Numbered tab dividers with at least 12 tabs.
- 3-hole punch
- Printer, Ink & Paper

I am going to break down each section in detail. However, here are the sections in my own Life Design Blueprint in outline form.

1. My Mission & Vision
2. Goal Setting
3. Progress Tracking & Habits
4. Planning & Scheduling
5. Budgeting & Investments
6. Books, Notes, Skills
7. Inspiration & Contributions
8. Ideas & Mind Maps
9. Health & Fitness

DETAILED SECTION BREAKDOWN

If you have the supplies you need already, then follow along with me. It will make more sense as we break down each section in detail.

If you don't have the supplies, then *get up* and go to the store and get them. I'll wait for you here, I promise! Or get on Amazon and order the supplies you need.

YOU MAY WANT TO QUIT READING RIGHT HERE

This book is all about taking action and making things happen in your life. If you thought you could quietly read this book and do nothing, then, my friend, you are wasting your time reading any further. Just give up, put this book back on the shelf or give it away because you are not an action taker and this entire formula is only for action takers and implementers. I do wish you the best of luck with all of your goals, but I most definitely want to save you the time and energy of reading any further.

If living the life you want to live is not worth a small investment in time, money and effort, then I have a sobering thought you may want to consider: life is going to be hard for you. I doubt anyone who's made it this far will fall into that category, but I just want to give you fair warning, that the rest of this chapter will break down specifically each part of the blueprint.

ALL RIGHT, LET'S MAKE SH*T HAPPEN!

The central concept of this book that makes it different from other books is that it goes beyond discussing theory. I want to help others take action and make shit actually happen! I created every single piece of this blueprint in downloadable and printable form so you don't have to try and figure out how to do this on your own. The "Blueprints" are constantly evolving and getting better as more and more people are sending me feedback on how things are working for them. I have a place for you to keep up with the progress and new versions here at:

WWW.MYLIFEDESIGNBLUEPRINT.COM/BLUEPRINTS

I want to disclose fully that I will just ask for your email address to access the over 37 downloadable and printable files that will make up your Life Design Blueprint. I promise I won't send you tons of annoying emails and you can opt out at any time. I am a hater of overly frequent emails myself and I know they get ignored and thrown away. I truly and sincerely want to stay in touch with those of you who actually take the journey and embark on this life-changing process with me, because helping others to achieve gives me incredible satisfaction and motivation. I cannot wait to hear your stories of massive success.

My Mission & Vision Section

TABLE OF CONTENTS FOR THIS SECTION

1. Personal Mission Statement: I'll show you mine, but you can read *The 7 Habits of Highly Effective People* for more details on how to write yours.

2. 30,0000-Foot Blueprint: Bird's-eye view of checkpoints during your lifetime.

3. Mindset Quotes. Words that get me in the right mindset for the day.

- 5 laws of stratospheric success from the *Go Giver* by Bob Burg and John David Mann

4. My Gratitude List: My running list of things I feel grateful for.

MY PERSONAL MISSION STATEMENT

Use the Personal Mission Statement Blueprint that can be found here at:

WWW.MYLIFEDESIGNBLUEPRINT.COM/BLUEPRINTS

I want to get personal with all of you and share my own personal mission statement, which I wrote back in January of 2016. This statement is sort of like my guiding light; I strive to align everything in my life to point in this direction. I read the book *The 7 Habits of Highly Effective People* in order to craft this as part of the actions the author encourages you to do. I want to encourage you to follow suit. It was hard initially, but the more I thought about what really mattered to me and what kind of life I wanted to live, the easier it became. This is what I came up with.

Here is my personal mission statement.

To live my life in the passionate pursuit of constant creation and continual growth in all areas. To be a genuine inspiration to others, proving that anything is possible if you will only put your mind to it. To create positive energy and creative solutions to problems that arise and to live my commitment of creating a life of abundance. To live my life fully without self-imposed limitations or the limitations of others, always encouraging others to reach for the stars. To show compassion for those less fortunate than me and to use my abundance to make a positive impact. To help elevate the minds and perspectives of human beings from all corners of the world through my various works and eventually commercial space flight.

I promise to do something special with my life.

Contributions I want to make

In the world: To inspire and help others recognize and achieve their wildest dreams. To have a lasting impact on those around me and for them to have lasting impact on those around them. To change the world in whatever way I can, lift and elevate people's perspective of our place in this world. I also want to be a part of the Mars colonization efforts.

In my family: To bring my family into a sustainable level of growth and success together as an interdependent unit. To love and listen and to be a blessing to them.

To my employees: To treat anyone I have direct influence over with dignity and respect, and empower them to be their best self. To encourage them to strive and reach for the stars and help them achieve their goals in life.

To my friends: To be a source of laughter and positive energy, to inspire, encourage and counsel friends in need and to enjoy and share life's greatest joys with those I call friend.

To my community: To be a source of inspiration and compassion. To invest in the lives of those around me.

How can you write yours?
For more detailed information on writing your Mission Statement, read *The 7 Habits of Highly Effective People* by Stephen R. Covey.

If you have not read this, then why not set it as a goal to read in the next month? This book started *everything* for me.

30,000-FOOT BLUEPRINT

Use the 30,000-Foot Blueprint that can be found here at:

WWW.MYLIFEDESIGNBLUEPRINT.COM/BLUEPRINTS

In this section, you basically list checkpoints in your life, describing what you would like to be, do and have. Think of this as an aerial view of your life from 30,000 feet.

Here are some samples of a 30,000-Foot Blueprint.

Checkpoint 1: I am making an additional $2,500 per month with no significant increase in my time obligations.

    I keep a minimum balance of ____in my savings account.

Checkpoint 2: I own a Tesla Model S and am halfway through paying my home off. I have started to look for and invest in real estate.

Checkpoint 3: I am married to a woman who is a genuine inspiration to me and we support each other's dreams.

    I own property outside of country I can visit three to five times per year for retreats and periods of reflection.

Checkpoint 4: I am generating over $____per month while working less than ____ hours per week. I am living in my purpose and doing the things I want to be doing with my time, such as _____ .

Hopefully, you get the point. This is just setting milestones and checkpoints for your life. The more specific you are, the better. Remember, we spoke earlier about externalizing your thoughts and envisioning your desired outcomes. This is one of the several ways we will do this in your Life Design Blueprint.

MINDSET QUOTES

Use the Mindset Quotes Blueprint you can download from HERE.

WWW.MYLIFEDESIGNBLUEPRINT.COM/BLUEPRINTS

This is where I keep powerful quotes that help get me ready for my day. Here are the ones on my list at the time of writing this book.

"The dreamers of the day are dangerous men, for they act on their dreams with open eyes to make them possible."
—T.E Lawrence

"People with goals are successful because they know where they are going."
—Earl Nightingale

"The only man who succeeds is the man who is progressively realizing a worthy ideal. He is the man that says I'm going to become this and then begins to work toward that goal. If you only care enough for a result, you will almost certainly attain it."
—Earl Nightingale

"Luck is what happens when preparation meets opportunity."
—Seneca

"What kind of world would this world be if everybody in it acted just like me?"
—Andy Andrews in The lost Choice

THE 5 LAWS OF STRATOSPHERIC SUCCESS

from the Go-Giver by Bob Burg, John David Mann

The Law of Value

How much more value you give than you take in payment.

The Law of Compensation

Income is determined by how many you serve and how well you serve them.

The Law of Influence

Influence is determined by how abundantly you place other people's interest first.

The Law of Authenticity

Be genuine. It is the most valuable gift you can offer.

The Law of Receptivity

The key to effective giving is to stay open to receiving.

MY GRATITUDE LIST

Use the Gratitude Blueprint you can download from HERE.

WWW.MYLIFEDESIGNBLUEPRINT.COM/BLUEPRINTS

Here are a few samples from my own gratitude list.

I am grateful to have smart, healthy, beautiful daughter.

I am grateful for the earth and the life it supports in a beautifully complex way.

I am grateful for the deep loving heart I have been given by my mother.

I am grateful for my father and his early words to me that inspired greatness in me.

I am grateful success can be attained by simply acting repeatedly on goals.

I am grateful for the wealth of books and knowledge people are willing to share with others.

I am grateful for_____.

What are you grateful for?

My list is over five pages and counting. I cannot explain to you how powerful keeping and reading over this list can be for your life. Having the feeling of genuine gratitude in your life will make it virtually impossible for you to be overwhelmed by negative emotions at the same time you are feeling deep gratitude. I like to think that I came up with this quote; however, chances are I heard it somewhere and I repeat it often: "gratitude will determine your latitude in life."

MY VISION BOARD

What do you want to be, do and have?

This can be a fun exercise and it may push you out of your comfort zone, which is where all your dreams start.

Go shopping for the car you want online. Look for the house, the property you want to live in. Go find the toys. Look at the places you want to visit, the experiences you want to live. Look at the contributions you want to make. Get visual and creative and put all of this here. You can cut out clippings from magazines and glue them on sheets of 3-hole punched paper or you can print out pictures and keep them here.

You can also create a physical vision board for your wall once you have collected your images of the lifestyle you want to live. Just go and buy cork board and pin it to your vision board.

Have fun with this. It can be very exciting actually doing this step once you get over thinking it's silly.

MOST IMPORTANTLY

It does not matter if you do not have the money or know how you will get these things for yourself. Don't let that negative voice in your mind tell you this is just fanciful dreaming and that you should skip this part. Make sure you do this. Don't overlook this powerful step. Having a visual representation will help you to envision your desired outcomes for your life.

Goal Setting Section

Use the included Goals Blueprint to help you come up with your goals for the year.

WWW.MYLIFEDESIGNBLUEPRINT.COM/BLUEPRINTS

I use the Tony Robbins method of deciding my first round of goals before I pair them up against each other in a showdown. I have found his method of devising meaningful goals to be the biggest benefit to this framework.

"Goals are dreams with a deadline."

—Tony Robbins

When Tony Robbins sets his goals, how does he do it? Robbins has devised a method to set big meaningful goals.

His approach will help you to feel motivated from the inside out and the whole process should take about 30–40 minutes. His way of designing goals will help you to create deeply inspiring goals related to the most important parts of your life.

In Robbins' book *Awaken the Giant Within*, he shares this goal-setting approach that he also teaches in his live seminars. Tony Robbins gives us a few tips to follow when doing this.

- **Write fast.** Robbins says, *"For each of these you'll have a period of time in which to brainstorm. Write rapidly–keep your pen moving, don't censor yourself, just get it all down on paper. Constantly ask yourself, what would I want for my life if I knew I could have it any way I wanted it?"*
- **Keep it simple.** Robbins says, *"Don't waste time getting overly specific with things like, 'I want a split-level house on time Nob Hill, in San Francisco.'"*
- **Be a kid.** Robbins says, *"Give yourself the freedom to explore the possibility of life without limits. Come up with a fun and outrageous list."*

Robbins organizes his goal setting into four different areas:

1. Personal development goals
2. Career/business/economic goals
3. Adventure goals and toys
4. Contribution goals

The point is to brainstorm in each of these four key areas rapidly for five minutes to generate your list. After that's done, you take one minute to decide a deadline for that goal. You also select one primary goal from each of those areas and you write about why it's so important to attain this goal. You should be spending only about eight minutes per goal area, so add that all up and it's equal to about 32 minutes. I would allow for a little bit of extra time.

Let's review in more detail each of the four areas of goals.

1. PERSONAL DEVELOPMENT GOALS

Step 1. Write down everything you'd like to improve related to your own personal growth. Spend five minutes doing this.

Summarized from *Awaken the Giant* by Tony Robbins:

> Write down everything you want to improve in your life that relates to your own growth as a person. How would you like to improve your body? Is there something you want to learn to do? What would you like to experience emotionally or master in your life?

Step 2. Set a timeline for each of your personal development goals. Spend one minute on this.

Put a 1 if it's one year or less, a 2 if it's two years, a 3 if it's three years, etc.

From *Awaken the Giant Within* by Tony Robbins:

> "Now that you've got your list of goals for your personal development that you can get excited about, take a minute now to give a timeline to each and every one of these. At this stage, it's not important to know how you're going to accomplish these goals."

Next, Robbins says the third step is to choose your most important one-year personal development goal and write about it for two minutes, describing why it's so important to you.

From *Awaken the Giant Within* by Tony Robbins:

> "Now choose your single most important one-year goal in this category—a goal that, if you were to accomplish it this year, would give you tremendous excitement and make you feel that the year was well invested. Take two minutes to write a

paragraph about why you are committed to achieving this goal within the year. Why is this compelling for you? What will you gain by achieving it?"

2. CAREER/BUSINESS/ECONOMIC GOALS

In this step, you follow the same pattern to set your career/business/economic goals.

Spend five minutes writing down anything and everything you can think of that you want related to your career, business or finances.

Step 2. Set a timeline to reach these goals. Spend one minute on this.

Put a 1 if it's one year or less, a 2 if it's two years, a 3 if it's three years, etc.

Step 3. Choose your most important one-year goal in this area and write about it for another two minutes, describing why it's so important to you and what you plan to do when you achieve this goal. It needs to be really compelling. Think deeply about why you want this.

3. ADVENTURE GOALS & TOYS

In this step, you decide the toys you want to have and the adventures you want to experience.

Step 1. Write down the adventures you want to go on and the toys you want have for five minutes. Remember, act as if there is no financial limit and anything is possible. Don't judge whether or not it's possible at this point. Manned mechanical flight was impossible until someone aspired to do it and figured out how to do it. Suspend your judgments for another time. Dream as a child dreams.

Step 2. Set a timeline for each of these goals. Spend only one minute doing this.

Now label them with numbers: 1=one year or less; 2=two years; 3=three years, etc.

Step 3. Choose your most important one-year adventure and toy goals and write for two minutes about why they are so important to you. If you keep asking yourself why you want something and you come up with a reason, then you ask yourself why that reason is important and keep doing that, you will eventually figure out the true reason you want something and often discover that what you really want is different than what you originally said you wanted.

Many people say they want to have $20 million, and when you ask them why, they say "because I want to be rich." Well, why do you want to be rich? They might say because I want to do what I want, when I want and how I want. That would be called freedom. What you really want is freedom, not $20 million. You can earn freedom for much less.

Asking yourself why will really help and is a critical part of the goal setting process. If you ignore this step, it's quite likely you won't have a good enough reason as to why you want that thing you think you want.

If you can't make your reason compelling, then choose another goal that excites and inspires you more. I can't stress to you enough how important this part is.

4. CONTRIBUTION GOALS

In this section, you write out all the ways you would like to contribute to the world around you.

Believe it or not, making a contribution is meaningful to people. In fact, making contributions is one of the six main human needs.

Step 1. Take five minutes to brainstorm your contribution goals.
From *Awaken the Giant Within* by Tony Robbins:

"These can be the most inspiring, compelling goals of all, because this is your opportunity to leave your mark, creating a legacy that makes a true difference in people's lives."

Step 2. Spend one minute setting a timeline for these goals.

By now, you should know the drill. Label them 1 for one year, 2 for two years, etc.

Step 3. Pick your most important one-year goal and write for two minutes about why this goal matters and why you need to attain it.

Remember, write down all the reasons you are absolutely committed to achieving it within the next year. If you can't come up with a good enough reason that truly inspires you, then choose another goal that excites you more.

SO HERE IS WHERE I PART FROM THE TONY ROBBINS METHOD

You now understand the Tony Robbins method of goal setting, and you can take this and apply it over and over in the different areas of your life. You should now have at least four major inspiring goals that will excite and inspire you for the entire year.

I'd love to say that this is all you have to do for this goal to become a reality, but that's not the case. There is more to it, and this is a major reason I wanted to develop this book. This is a great method of setting your goals, but how do you actually attain those goals?

Starting with the strongest possible reason is critical. Without this critical step, doing the harder parts to reach these goals will most likely not be possible for you, so follow this process to set your goals. I will further explain how to take all of this and put it into action.

The main points are: 1) externalizing your thoughts on paper and 2) engaging in serious critical thinking to determine which goals are important and why. These are the *key* takeaways I want to emphasize here.

There is a Goal Setting Blueprint download available **HERE** to help you with this process.

WWW.MYLIFEDESIGNBLUEPRINT.COM/BLUEPRINTS

Define and Envision

Take the time to go through the blueprint I provided to you at the link above. This will give you a framework to follow in order to help you define your reasons and to begin envisioning the outcome. Like I said before, this book is all about action taking and the reason I do not include the entire process here is that it would require more space than is available in this book. You also need to take an actual action in order to get yourself in the habit of doing what it takes to reach your goals. By clicking on the link and printing a set of blueprints you can fill out, you'll be taking a positive step in the right direction, which makes you different from 99% of readers who are not action takers.

THE MONEY MAKER RIGHT HERE: DEFINE THE KEY HABITS

After you have come up with your major goals in the major areas of your life, then you're ready for the big boss secret sauce of the entire process, which will help you to put these goals on autopilot. This involves breaking your goals down into the right habits that will help you achieve them.

Use the downloadable Habit Creation Blueprint Worksheet. Find it **HERE.**

WWW.MYLIFEDESIGNBLUEPRINT.COM/BLUEPRINTS

If your goal is to lose 40 pounds within six months, this could prove to be very difficult if you don't break the interim goals down properly.

Think about some key habits you could create that will support your goal.

- Weigh yourself every day and record the number.
- Do 10–15 minutes of exercise each day, no matter what.
- Eat something healthy before bed instead of sweets.

You may need to focus on creating more than one key habit that will support this goal. Many experts will tell you not to try to form more than one habit at a time, but I disagree. We have formed dozens of daily habits without really thinking about them. In my opinion, the key is to find ways to trigger and replace old habits with new ones that support and align with the goals that you decided were super important to you.

Remember, you don't need to have superhuman willpower, only just *enough* to form a habit.

Start with a small habit. It might just be the catalyst domino that will start to knock over the other larger dominos in your life that will lead to much larger success.

I'll admit this was hard for me, so I want to help you with the process.

If your goal is to write a book, then here are some sample habits you could create.

Write at least 200 words per day every day.

Even if you typed at a slow speed of 11 words per minute, it would only require 18 minutes of typing per day. That is perfectly doable if you have a truly meaningful reason you want to write a book to share with the world. If you think 18 minutes is too much to dedicate every day for 61 days, then it may mean your goal of writing a book doesn't have a truly compelling reason behind it, and you should revisit the goal setting process.

This is okay. Sometimes, we think that we want something, but then we later find out we really didn't want that thing. It's totally okay to change your mind and make adjustments.

Remember what my mentor Jimmy taught me: you have to pay the price!

Here are a few more habits you could focus on that would support the goal of writing a book.

Commit to taking an online course on writing and complete 10–15 minutes of the course every day.

Get creative and hack these habits if you have to.

Record yourself talking and have the audio transcribed. There are inexpensive service providers that can transcribe the audio and even some speech recognition software that could help make the physical writing process easier.

Remember that we talk differently then we write and you will have to edit the transcripts quite a bit.

Let's break down some more goals to help you with this.

Goal: Grow my professional network.
Habit: Reach out to one new person a day. In one year, that's 365 new people.

Goal: Improve my relationship with my significant other.
Habit: Tell them how much you appreciate them every day.

Goal: Stop procrastinating.

Habit: Write out the steps for what you need to do; then time-block your day and work on only one thing at a time.

Procrastination is a big problem that I believe this Life Design Blueprint will help you conquer. If you have made it this far and are still procrastinating, then bravo for your determination, but get up and go order the stuff you need or go to the store and get started!

PICK "THE TWELVE"

If defining habits was the big boss secret sauce, then this next part is his little minion who turns everything he touches into gold.

Here you will use the 12 Habits Blueprint to help you with this step.

WWW.MYLIFEDESIGNBLUEPRINT.COM/BLUEPRINTS

You're going to take your top habits that you decided to focus on creating, and narrow that list down to the most important 12. They need to be very specific actions you can quickly check off as you complete them.

This was one of the most valuable steps for me because it set up the framework that I am about to get into regarding progress tracking.

Progress Tracking & Habits Section

From your list of 12 habits, you will now be able to fill out this next blueprint.

Here you will use the 12 Habits Tracker Blueprint to help you with this step.

WWW.MYLIFEDESIGNBLUEPRINT.COM/BLUEPRINTS

You will use this to simply mark off when each of those predetermined 12 habits have been completed for the day. I'll give you a secret tip I used.

I made using my Life Design Blueprint one of those 12 habits to check in the morning and in the evening before I went to bed. I considered this just one habit.

This single piece of paper created so many results for me. I was able to see my physical progress each day. I would be excited to check off one of my habits, and I'd often find myself looking at it more often than just two times per day. This was really helpful because it would remind me of what I still had time to do in the day.

This entire process became a game I would play with myself. Seeing the x's marked on my habit tracking blueprint gave me a small sense of satisfaction, but as the days went on, the satisfaction grew because I could see actual progress.

THE WEEKLY GOALS AND REVIEW

As mentioned before, setting goals properly is important, but there is more to it than that. In addition to setting goals, you need to review and reflect regularly so that you can adjust course as needed. Think of a ship leaving a boatyard and trying to make it across the entire ocean. They have to make course adjustments frequently during the trip because being just a few degrees off at the start, without any corrections, could mean reaching the wrong continent at the end of the voyage.

Use the Weekly Goals & Review Blueprint to help you with this.

WWW.MYLIFEDESIGNBLUEPRINT.COM/BLUEPRINTS

This is where you:

- Set your main goals for the week
- Break down the steps to reach them
- Review what you learned at weeks end
- List the major wins you have had
- Review lessons you will apply moving forward into the next week

You may be thinking, hey, wait a minute!

Shouldn't this go in the goals section?

Put it wherever you want. For me, it goes in the progress tracking and habits section. This is my favorite section because I can see so much progress happening here.

The point is: this is **YOUR LIFE DESIGN BLUEPRINT**. I'm giving you a framework that you can use, copy and improve upon as you go— once you understand the entire process. I found so much value in it that I wanted to share it. If you discover a better way, I would love to hear about it.

At the end of each week, you will set aside some time. I usually set aside a few hours in the evening on a Sunday after a relaxing family day to review and go over my weekly goals. I write down the wins, losses and lessons learned for the week. I think about how I can improve moving forward, and I see where maybe my weekly goals were not fully aligned and supporting my larger goals. This is where I do those course corrections I was talking about earlier.

THE MONTHLY PROGRESS TRACKER BLUEPRINT

This one is simple. It's a straightforward way to see if you are making progress on your year's goals.

Use the Monthly Progress Tracker Blueprint.

WWW.MYLIFEDESIGNBLUEPRINT.COM/BLUEPRINTS

This part should be very self-explanatory. If you made even a little progress on that goal during the month, put a checkmark for the month during your end-of-month review.

After doing four weekly reviews at the end of the month, a few days before month's end, I will take an hour or so to review all four weeks and look for any patterns or more adjustments I need to make. This is another chance to make further course corrections, setting me up to make even more progress moving into my next month.

I consolidate all of my wins, lessons learned and things I'm grateful for onto one sheet. I put in the very end of this month. This makes it easy to see how far you really came that month.

Human beings have a tendency to remember the bad things and ignore the good things. We don't give ourselves enough credit for all the things we accomplish simply because we haven't reached our finish line yet. Our brains are actually wired this way to highlight the negative things. Back in caveman times, this helped us to identify patterns and protect ourselves from dangerous situations. Today it can hurt us. Seeing continual progress will help you maintain a positive attitude, and make you feel like you're really moving your life in a new direction that excites you.

Don't lie to yourself. Sometimes, we're going to eat sh*t and fall down.

Let's not be naïve. Sometimes, we fail, but remember that failure is the mother of all success. While highlighting your wins and successes is valuable, going over and reviewing your failures can be even more valuable. It gives us a new framework and a way to deal with our failures.

Failure always feels bad, but this process takes failure and reframes it as one of the most valuable activities you can do for yourself.

FAILURE IS YOUR FRIEND

Use the Reframe Failure Blueprint.

WWW.MYLIFEDESIGNBLUEPRINT.COM/BLUEPRINTS

We have a tendency to avoid talking about our failures, yet we let them dominate our minds and affect our thoughts and feelings about ourselves. This makes us less effective than we could be. By asking questions and carefully picking out the insights and lessons our failures can teach us, we can arm ourselves with a new approach. One of my best friends, Ryan Reed, is a talented writer and leader who I served with in the Marine Corps. He sends me a text with some motivational saying almost every day. He recently sent one that I later discovered Henry Ford coined. Ford said, "Failure is the opportunity to begin again more intelligently." The quote was significant to me because it came at the same moment when some things that I had been working on didn't turn out as planned.

This time, I handled my disappointment differently. I don't know whether to attribute it to my improving meditation practice or recently discovering float therapy. I highly recommend trying float therapy, also called sensory deprivation tanks. The benefits are unreal! I'll share more on this later in the book.

I was able to simply look at this setback from the outside and think, "Okay, where is the lesson here? What did I do wrong? How can I improve next time?" It immediately became something positive, and I was grateful for the experience. I didn't feel down or discouraged for more than a few moments. I was able to learn from this, then readjust and rapidly try again. This is when I came up with the idea for the failure blueprint. This whole mental process was so valuable to me that I knew it could help others, so I added this to my Life Design Blueprint.

It's a simple process. It asks a series of questions that will help you to think and review where you went wrong and how you can reframe this negative into a positive experience that leads you forward instead of setting you back in life.

CAVEMAN SYNDROME

Our brains are programmed to notice negative things. We were wired like that for survival, but today this mental pattern can hurt us. When things don't go our way, we can often fall into slumps and overreact. We think it's the end of the world when, in reality, if you look at the worst-case scenario, it could've been much worse. It's not the end of the world. You will still be okay if you pay the rent a few days late, or if someone you had deep feelings for breaks up with you. You're going to be fine. If you use the failure blueprint, it's going to help you to reframe the setback into your comeback.

Planning, Scheduling and Travel

I used to dread planning and scheduling, but then I learned that systems create freedom.

Here is an outline of the Life Design Blueprint pages contained in this section.

- Month at a glance
- Week at a glance
- Weekly routine
- The daily plan
  - o I'll show you my favorite method that works best for me.
- Project Plan Blueprint
- Travel Plan Blueprint

MONTH AT A GLANCE

Use the Month at a Glance Blueprint.

WWW.MYLIFEDESIGNBLUEPRINT.COM/BLUEPRINTS

Narrow in on your top three or four goals for the month that support your larger 90-day and one-year goals and put them in the provided areas in this section. If you're following along, it would be helpful for you to be looking at this sheet while reading these section descriptions.

Next, list your major to-dos for the month. Be sure not to put too many to-do items here. Just list the major ones that are really important, perhaps even critical, to the completion of the major goals you selected for the month.

Now, we move on to your big appointments and events you need to remember for the month, followed by major bills and the dates you need to pay them by.

Lastly, there is an area for an end-of-month review. In this section, list what has worked for during the month. What did not work so well? What could you do more of? What should you do less of? This may seem redundant since similar items are covered in your weekly and monthly review. However, approach it as a secondary opportunity to catch things you didn't catch in that section. You will find quite often that you have additional insights after looking at this outline of a schedule. Did this schedule reflect and line up with the goals you set for your week? It should have because you used your weekly goal setting blueprint to create your rough schedule. If you did not, then you will understand why you may not have moved as far as you would have liked toward achieving your goal. In this Life Design Blueprint, every section has other sections that share an interdependent relationship. It's the combination of the sections and the rationale behind completing those sections that keep you on track toward massive progress.

WEEK AT A GLANCE

Use the Week at a Glance Blueprint.

WWW.MYLIFEDESIGNBLUEPRINT.COM/BLUEPRINTS

In this section, you will narrow down your top three or four goals for the week, remembering that they should align with your goals for the month. Having this interdependent series of connected but broken-down goals will all but ensure you reach your goals. As long as you started with the first input into this loop, the proper habits, you will make steady progress toward your goals.

Just as in the month at a glance, here you will list your major to-dos for the week and break things down further by the day. I actually used this section to plan out the creation of my very first Life Design Blueprint.

For example, on Monday, you could list "buy all supplies needed for Life Design Blueprint" and "finish key habits." On Tuesday, you could include "fill out habit tracker." On Wednesday, "finish weekly goals blueprint." You get the picture.

FOR THOSE WHO HATE DAILY PLANNERS

I discovered a very simple way to plan out my days. Here's a quick summary.

I review the previous week on Sundays in the evening, as I mentioned earlier. At this same time, I plan and map out my coming week. In less than two hours, I can review the week before and plan the next one. This weekly planning is *monumental* in terms of my ability to handle things smoothly as they come up during the week. I take the time to plan so that I have a road map and guide for what I need to be focused on to get me where I want to go.

I use mind maps to plan my week. It's so simple and helps me to visually see and map things out. My favorite way to mind map is with an app called Mindmeister. You can collaborate with others on the same mind map and you can link mind maps together. This allows me to access it on any device. My favorite two ways to use it are with a keyboard on a computer and on my iPad with a Bluetooth keyboard attached. It makes mind mapping so easy and simple. I literally mind map everything. I'm in the process of mind mapping 200 books for this year because one of my goals is to read 200 books. I found that mind mapping 200 books would allow me to more effectively retain and recall the information. Notebooks are cool, but there's no way for me to easily reference my handwritten mind maps, particularly when I'm traveling. Mind mapping truly has revolutionized my ability to plan things and strategically think about my plans.

Here is my method for planning out my week with mind mapping. It's simple.

I created a mind map to time-block my days into sections such as morning, midday, afternoon, evening and before bed. It looks like this.

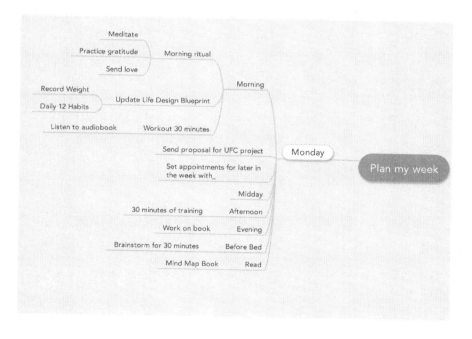

I can do this quickly and see things visually, and then I can reference this and use it to fill out my week at a glance section. I even now combine every week of a month on a single mind map, which makes looking at an entire month in a new visual way so much easier for me.

Your mind map never runs out of space. You can zoom in and out and move it around, but it keeps everything connected and relating to each other visually. For me, it's like my secret weapon for how I can be so precise and productive. Digital mind mapping is in my foreseeable future. I'm imagining digital mind maps in virtual reality. How awesome would that be! I'm sure it's coming. I may even create a business opportunity out of that myself. Augmented reality mind mapping could one day replace boring meeting rooms with whiteboards. You could meet and create in an open space and collaborate with others.

PLANNING VIA CALENDAR APPS

Using the above process to time-block your day is super effective. I take it a step further and input everything into my Google calendar app so that my days are blocked off and I can see it. This is a super-slick, easy-to-use visual format on my phone.

I actually plan out two weeks ahead of time because I spend a significant amount of time determining my strategic performance indicators along with the tasks and processes that are attached to them.

You can use this Blueprint here to use this method of planning if you want to supercharge your productivity.

WWW.MYLIFEDESIGNBLUEPRINT.COM/BLUEPRINTS

CREATING PERFORMANCE INDICATORS AND TASKS TO REACH THEM

Your goals are the results you want to reach. This is your end point.

This goal should be something that is very tangible and measurable like a specific amount of money, or the completion of a task.

Here's how this looks.

If you pick something tangible that has a lot of meaning for you and can be completed in 90 days, this will generate excitement in your life.

Performance indicators lead you toward your goal.

Think of it like this. Making improvements and measuring those improvements will create constant progress and help you reach your goal.

Remember when I said we're going to break everything down into 90 days and then those 90 days into two-week increments? This is where this becomes really important.

Let's take the following example.

Your overall goal for the year is to earn $100,000.
That would mean that your:
90-day goal is to earn $25,000
One-month goal: $8,333.33
Two-week goal: $4,166

You may look at this and think, okay, well, I broke it down; that still does not tell me how to do this.

First of all, if you don't have a strategy or a way of earning extra money, then you have to start there first. If you don't currently have a way to earn extra money, what do you do?

You would set a different goal. For example: I want to add two additional streams of income into my life over the next 90 days that will earn me, by year's end, a combined income of $100,000 this year.

Your performance indicator would be set like this.

I will increase the number of streams of income I have from just one to three within the next two weeks. Be sure to set an actual date.

You can then break down this performance indicator into the *how*.

You would list the different tasks you would have to accomplish in order to meet this performance indicator.

For this example, some tasks would include:

1. Identify and make a list of potential income streams
2. Pick 10 options on the list to do more research on
3. Narrow the list down to the top five options with the potential for me to earn the extra income I want
4. Pick the best two of those options

These tasks and processes need to be as specific as you can make them. Make sure you cover all the bases of what you are doing, when you are doing it, where you are doing it at and why you are doing it. This helps to create absolute clarity and helps you to avoid procrastination due to confusion or lack of direction.

These tasks are what you will actually put into your calendar. This is how I would write the above examples into my calendar. I literally do this in my Google calendar. It seems like a lot of effort, but let me tell you how amazing it is to wake up and be able to know what needs to be done, where, when and why. This gave me a new feeling of freedom and control over my life's direction.

For the first example, here's what I would write, following the formula of **what + when + where + why**

1. I will make a list of 20 different potential income streams on Friday and I will save this list as a Google spreadsheet in my financial ideas folder. I am doing this to narrow down the best options for reaching my goal of earning $100,000 this year.

2. I will spend no more than 15 minutes on Saturday researching each option on my list and narrowing it down to the ones that interest me the most. I will do more research on at least 10 options. I will save links and notes in my Evernote app under the extra income notebook. I am doing this to get closer to picking my final few options that I will pursue in order to reach my goal of earning $100,000 this year.

By now, you should understand the level of depth and the formula to use to determine which actions you should be doing to reach your performance indicators that will, in turn, lead you to your goals.

MY WEEKLY ROUTINES

Remove the clutter from your mind, such as the things that you need to do every week. Our brains should be used for thinking about things like solving problems and working things out, not thinking of all the everyday things we need to remember and do. This is externalization in practice again. By removing the routine things you know you need to do every single week from your mind, you can free up that mental space to be more clear and handle things more effectively. This has helped me to focus, and it helps me avoid worrying about things because I know I can just look here and see what I need to do.

- I do laundry on this day
- I review my week and plan the next one on Sunday evenings
- I have lunch with my friends on this day
- I take my dry cleaning in on this day
- What do you do every week that you could get out of your mind?

The point is to remove the burden of remembering these things and put them here. We use this method in other sections of this Life Design Blueprint as well.

THE DAILY PLAN

As I've said before, I'm not a huge fan of planning things down to the minute. I've included several methods of planning your day that should be very self-explanatory.

You can find the Daily Plan Blueprint HERE in multiple versions. One may work better for you.

WWW.MYLIFEDESIGNBLUEPRINT.COM/BLUEPRINTS

I already shared with you my absolute favorite way to plan my day and get the *right* things done in a day.

- Time blocking with mind maps
- Google calendar activities in blocks of time

THE PROJECT PLAN BLUEPRINT

When taking on any new project, taking the time to make a plan can save you so much time and effort and help you to accomplish much more than you thought you could. I will go through a sample project plan here.

Use the Project Plan Blueprint Worksheet to help you do this.

WWW.MYLIFEDESIGNBLUEPRINT.COM/BLUEPRINTS

Imagine the project you need to complete is cleaning out the garage, but you have been putting it off for months.

Project name: Operation Remove Clutter.

Summary of project: Remove all the relics and clutter from the garage.

Break it down into main steps:

- Sort what can stay and what must go
- Throw away useless items
- Take pictures of what you can sell and post it online

Why and how this will improve my life:

- I can have room for a weight bench.
- My wife will love me today for it. I have space to work on my _____

Super helpful tip!

Knowing *why* you need to do something and *how* it will improve your life will make doing things so much easier. Here are just a few of the benefits I have noticed using this method.

- Will make you more motivated to actually complete it.
- Will help fight procrastination.
- Can also show you that it's not a project you need or want to do.
  - Allows you to not waste time on pointless projects.

THE TRAVEL PLAN

Use the Travel Plan Blueprint.

WWW.MYLIFEDESIGNBLUEPRINT.COM/BLUEPRINTS

Trips you want to take are often put on the back burner. This will help you to make those trips a reality for yourself! It's a simple yet powerful concept that I have used to plan trips I didn't think I would be able to take. Once I did this travel plan blueprint, it made the trip attainable for me, and I hope it can do the same for you too. Travel is one of those things that people sadly look at as a luxury. Traveling has the power to inspire and help us grow by exposing us to different cultures and locations and experiences. Traveling to places you want to visit can create such satisfaction and feelings of enjoyment that you should most definitely make more time to travel where you want with the people you want. It's a myth that traveling is too expensive and only for the wealthy. There is a great book about traveling the world on a budget called *How to Travel the World on $50 a Day* by Matt Kepnes.

I especially believe it to be more important than ever to travel today with the increased fear in the world. It will truly open your eyes once you see the world and experience its people, and how wonderful and beautiful the people of this world really can be, and how our way of doing things in America is not the only way. You may even discover that our way is not the best way, and you may enjoy the way other people do things.

Polarized points of view in politics lead to what's called confirmation bias. We tend to look for things that confirm our beliefs and ignore anything that contradicts them. This leads to people becoming even more polarized. Have you ever wondered why talking politics gets so heated between people who consider themselves to be civilized? Before you start judging, I am neither Republican nor Democrat; however, I want to use this as an example to illustrate my point as it relates to why we should travel more.

Republicans will listen to news stations and sources that align with their beliefs, finding liberal media to be "repulsive and manipulative" whereas Democrats will avoid Republican-flavored media and news because it's "bigoted and bashes the poor."

Of course, some of these stereotypes have some degree of truth to them when seen from the opposing point of view, but neither side likes to objectively take in the other point of view. If we only consume news and information from media outlets and other sources we tend to agree with, we have no objectivity and no accurate way to assess the issues of the day in a balanced and logical way. This is why traveling outside of your state and country can open up your mind to an entirely different world that you have not experienced before. I believe that parents should travel with their children as often as possible. Our planet does not have real lines in the dirt where one country ends and another begins. We are all connected and what happens in one place can affect what happens in another. We are in an interdependent system. No matter what your political beliefs are, this is a reality that we cannot change.

Traveling to other countries and meeting the people, and seeing that they are just people like you and me, will make it much harder to push hateful agendas or projects that hurt others for the benefit of the few.

In this travel blueprint, you will:

Break down the costs.

- Airfare
- Transportation
- Accommodations
- Food
- Entertainment

Brainstorm the adventure.

- Where do you want to go?
- What do you want to do?
- What do you want to see?
- What would you like to experience?

Divide the costs by the number of months remaining until the planned date of the trip.

Arrive at an amount you need to save to make it happen.

MAKE A PROMISE to yourself to MAKE IT HAPPEN!

Budgeting and Finances

What gets measured gets managed. Keeping a close eye on your finances will help you to grow and manage your money more effectively.

In this section, we will cover the following blueprints:

- My Money Opportunities
- My Budget & Expenses
- Income Tracker
- Expense Tracker

MY MONTHLY BUDGET & EXPENSES

Use the Monthly Budget Blueprint Worksheet.

WWW.MYLIFEDESIGNBLUEPRINT.COM/BLUEPRINTS

What are your sources of income? List them here.

What is your income goal for the month?

What is the difference between how much you want and how much you're actually earning?

List your expenses. Yes, list them all. It makes you think twice about what you're actually spending money on.

- Go over your expenses once every week or every two weeks.
- Total the difference between your income and your expenses.
- If you have too much "month at the end of your money," then this will help you identify why.
- This was initially hard for me since I managed everything through online banking.
- Writing them out works because it forces you to pay attention to the numbers.

BILL PAYMENT CHECKLIST

Knowing which bills are due and when, as well as if you have paid them, is helpful in removing stress and uncertainty.

It also helps with planning out expenses. The less you have to figure in your mind, the freer you will feel. Don't underestimate how powerful this can be.

Use the Bill Payment Checklist Worksheet.

WWW.MYLIFEDESIGNBLUEPRINT.COM/BLUEPRINTS

OPPORTUNITIES BLUEPRINT

Use the Opportunities Blueprint.

WWW.MYLIFEDESIGNBLUEPRINT.COM/BLUEPRINTS

In this section, you can write down potential new income streams.

Write down when you hear someone say I would pay money for____.

- Ideas for products or services you think of in a moment of need.
- Talents you have that you could teach.
- Things collecting dust you can sell.
- Skills you can acquire and sell.

The point is to put it down on paper. It may strike you later, when going through this section, that you have a viable option that you would have forgotten about had you not written it down. This section has made me money!

INVESTING IN YOUR WEALTH

Two absolutely incredible books on building wealth and developing the right mindset around money that absolutely changed my life are: *The Secrets of the Millionaire Mind* by T. Harv Eker and *The Richest Man in Babylon* by George Clason.

If you seriously desire to improve your financial well-being and build wealth, I strongly recommend these books.

You can find a booklist at www.mylifedesignblueprint.com/readinglist

The next two sections are super simple.

Use the Income Tracker and Expense Tracker Worksheets.

WWW.MYLIFEDESIGNBLUEPRINT.COM/BLUEPRINTS

INCOME TRACKER

Where you keep track of the incoming money.

EXPENSE TRACKER

Where you keep track of the money that is going out.

Learning & Skills

MY LEARNING BLUEPRINT

This section is also one of my favorites. I think of this as sort of like shopping on Amazon for any skill I want to develop. All I have to do is figure out which skills I will need to achieve the goals I want, then it's almost as simple as ordering them with a single click.

Many people mortgage their futures by paying for traditional education and getting expensive degrees. While they do have value, it is my opinion that this value is overstated and many degree programs lack innovation. Traditional forms of education are not the future; the future is self-education. As my mentor Jim Rohn said, "Formal education will make you a living; self-education will make you a fortune."

We now have easy access to world-class teachers, coaches, trainers and instructors teaching anything and everything you could ever want to learn. This gives those with the ability to be self-directed learners an edge over their counterparts who rely on expensive degrees.

In *The Personal MBA* by Josh Kaufman, he makes the bold claim that:

"MBA programs are a waste of time and money. Even the elite schools offer outdated assembly-line educations about profit-and-loss statements and PowerPoint presentations. After two years poring over sanitized case studies, students are shuffled off into middle management to find out how business *really* works."

This seems to be a recurring theme heard I've heard from a variety of experienced professionals. While there are undeniable benefits to the networking opportunities and having that fancy degree on your resume, many people are discovering that the cost is much too high.

The stress of having debt hangs over you for years after you finish school. This is something that challenges millions of people today. With a little bit of self-directed and determined effort, you can cherry-pick the skills and knowledge you need to live the type of life you want, both degree-free and debt-free.

It is my firm belief that if education organizations do not become more flexible in offering a customized and self-directed form of study, then more and more people will turn to other alternatives. You can make great money, own your own business, work for great companies and live a full and satisfying life all without going into serious debt and mortgaging your life for possibly a decade to earn an assembly-line degree.

Obviously, there are certain professions that will always require some form of rigid study. However, as we adapt to a new global economy, the pressure for most to compete with their worldwide counterparts will only increase, and job markets will shrink as artificial intelligence (AI) technology inevitably replaces large sectors of jobs. Not enough people are considering that this could be a real possibility in the near future. The speed at which AI is evolving and the types of jobs it will render obsolete could really create some economic struggles for those who are caught unaware after it's too late. If AI replaces your industry, you will still have to pay back the loans you received for the degree that you can no longer use. Remember to think proactively and look at developing trends in the industries you want to move into. Don't fall prey to slick marketing tactics that sell you certainty in a world where *nothing* is certain.

SELF-DIRECTION AND YOUR LEARNING BLUEPRINT

If you can develop a plan for the skills, knowledge and abilities that you will need to live the kind of life you want to live, then, as I said before, you can almost literally order skills from Amazon. Books that contain decades and even centuries worth of curated knowledge from practicing experts in their respective fields can give you key insights into what is truly important to know in order to work in that field or industry. This will not apply to every single type of industry. However, chances are that you can learn more from those who have come before us, who spent the money on the degrees and who can give us shortcuts to lessons they learned through trial and error.

Let's take the film industry, for example. While many filmmakers swear by what film school did for them, there is an equal number who will laugh or cry and tell you how much money they wasted on their degrees. There are countless lower-cost options where you can gain the same knowledge and avoid years of trial and error.

I will refrain from beating this dead horse too many more times, but you can probably tell I am a believer in self-directed education. The most successful people I know do not have degrees and speak openly about not needing one.

This approach will not work for everyone. It does take a certain amount of strategy and discipline. If you have the ability to put together this Life Design Blueprint for your life and turn it into a system that will work for you, then chances are you have what it takes to be self-directed enough to cut your learning-to-earning time in half.

For my next trick, I won't be teaching you how to skip eight years of graduate studies to become a doctor, but I will share with you something that has helped me acquire important skills and abilities.

Use the Learning Blueprint.

WWW.MYLIFEDESIGNBLUEPRINT.COM/BLUEPRINTS

Let's start by picking the top five to 10 skills you want to learn for the year.

List the courses you can take or the books you can read to learn these skills. You may need to do a fair amount of research to find the right sources you want to learn from.

It helps if you break things down and simplify what you want to learn. See the example below.

I want to learn how to network better.

A book you could read is: *How to Win Friends and Influence People.* There is no shortage of incredible books that can provide valuable insights. To learn this on your own, it could take a lifetime of trial and error.

DECONSTRUCTION

Deconstruct complex abilities into smaller skills. Breaking it down will help, for example, if you want to learn photography.

You could break things down into smaller skills.

- Learn the basics of photography.
- Learn about digital cameras.
- Learn about lighting.
- Learn about photo editing software.

This is why I said before that we can almost click and order the skills we want to learn. Through classes, online training and books, you can learn anything and everything you can think of, from digital photography to how to write your own business plan. The internet is an amazing place full of nearly limitless information, yet so many people waste their time by using the internet for entertainment only.

THE COST OF YOUR DREAMS

In about the same amount of time you spend watching reruns on Netflix, you could learn the skills you need to earn six figures or more. Instead of scrolling endlessly through memes and videos on Facebook, what if you applied that time to learning skills that would take you to the place you want to be in your life? Would that be worth the small sacrifice? For me, this a no-brainer.

I do not even have a television in my room, nor do I spend more than one hour a week watching entertaining shows. I will even go months without watching any at all. For me, learning and growing and making progress on my goals and helping others consumes me and brings me great satisfaction. I do enjoy TV shows and movies. I just use on-demand services on the weekend and not before I have met my critical goals for the week. This won't work for everyone as not everyone will be willing to pay the price for what they want, but it works for me.

I have gained such power over my life by strictly controlling what reaches my eyes and ears. I completely eliminated any form of broadcast news exposure because it is almost all biased toward negativity, drama and conflict, polarizing our population and making us more and more afraid of each other.

After I stopped listening to any kind of news, I started to feel better about the world around me and about other people. My mood improved significantly.

At any given moment, there are countless amazing things going on, people helping people, massive improvements in technology that might help billions of people on this planet. Too many people are concerned with the fact that this celebrity got another DUI or that this political party is doing this reprehensible thing that you disagree with. There are other ways to stay informed and plugged into events that are important to you without having to subject yourself to the propaganda of today's style of news reporting.

Give this a try: stop listening to the news for a week or two and see how it changes your overall perception of the world around you.

GETTING THROUGH THE WITHDRAWALS

Once you have been taken a break from the news for a period of time, when you finally do hear the news or see headlines, you will begin to notice things you never noticed before. Listen to the language they use and the statements they are making. They are basically in the business of telling people exactly what to think and how to feel about the subject they are reporting on, depending on which news station you are listening to.

Liberal and conservative news organizations will present the same story with different facts that support only their point of view. There is little objectivity. To get closer to the truth, you could compare both versions of the same story, which takes a tremendous amount of energy to do. To me, it's just not worth it. I'm happier when I can remove this negative influence from my life and focus on improving myself and the lives of those around me. The truth is that you can't care about everything equally. We have limited attention and energy. I think that staying aware of important issues and topics can be done in a much more positive way.

Some people may take a hard stance against what I am saying here and that is perfectly fine. I will not try to impose my way of thinking on you. I am merely sharing something that has significantly improved the quality of my life and the lives of the people that I know who have done away with this kind of negative input. Remember, garbage in, garbage out. What we feed our minds is ultimately the basis for what forms our thoughts. Your mind is like a factory and the things you allow to enter your mind are the ingredients that the factory will use to create your life. Do you think that you can live a prosperous, satisfying life if all you constantly feed your mind is negative garbage? I would say absolutely not.

OUR PERCEPTIONS CAN BE BIASED BASED ON INTRODUCTIONS

There have been studies on how our perceptions are altered depending on how something or someone is introduced to us. If someone new was introduced to you by someone you already knew and they said that this person was a brilliant person, you would be more likely to see them the way they were described to you initially. Conversely, if they were introduced to you in a negative light, chances are you would be more suspicious and possibly even feel negatively about the person. This has been tested extensively in various audiences, and it's clear that the way something is presented to you can and does have a direct effect on how you perceive a person or idea.

BOOKS ARE THE SECRET WEAPON OF THE WEALTHY

Will Smith says the keys to life are running and reading. I agree with the reading part! It has been reported that Warren Buffett reads up to eight hours a day. Why do you think this is?

The most successful people are often avid readers. If you want the quickest route to a more successful and fulfilling life, read as if your life depended on it.

- Lifetimes of knowledge can be gained from a few hundred pages.
- Imagine a book as a conversation between you and the author.
- Books are my mentors.
- Write all over and in your books.
- You don't need to read books cover to cover.
- Read with an intention, such as "How to deal with people you can't stand."

- Audiobooks are wonderful and can help tremendously.

Keep a list of books you want to read, recommended books or books you would recommend to others.

Use the My Book List Blueprint Worksheet.

WWW.MYLIFEDESIGNBLUEPRINT.COM/BLUEPRINTS

LIFE HACK ALERT

I digitally mind map any book I am reading to better retain, recall and use the knowledge. Taking notes is good, but I find that creating mind maps of books helps me to take notes faster while clearly understanding concepts and ideas better. It gives me the ability to visually reference the material quickly and in a connected way that note taking on paper or in typed documents just can't compare to.

I can quickly recall complex information from books and use my mind maps to apply the knowledge and insights effectively. I take this extra step when reading or listening to an audiobook because it's infinitely more valuable to me to if I can recall and use the information at a later date. I no longer have to flip through volumes of different notebooks searching for the exact information I need because I can easily see it on my digital mind map in a visually structured way. Here's an example of what one of my mind maps looks like for a book.

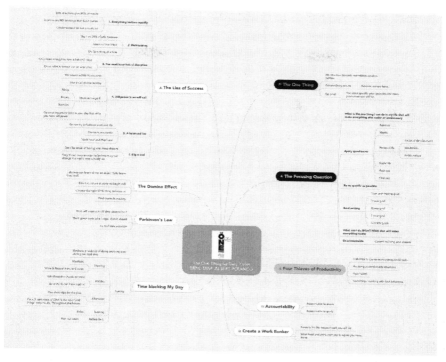

Inspiration & Contribution

WHAT INSPIRES YOU?

Keep anything that inspires you here in this section. It could be anything.

- Quotes
- Art
- Magazine clippings
- Pictures of people, places or things
- Advertisements for toys you want
- Drawings
- Anything that makes you feel inspired

Get creative with this section. Make it yours!

Having a collection of sources for inspiration is helpful and can remind you of why something is important to you when facing challenges.

WHAT DO YOU WANT TO CONTRIBUTE?

Think about what you want to give to others, how you want to help causes that matter to you.

List ways you want to contribute.

- Help feed the homeless and less fortunate.
- Donate to the _____ charity for _____.
- Give away my old clothing.
- Donate my time to _____ cause.
- Teach my dad how to use a modern cell phone.
- Improve someone's life in some way.

If you can forget for a moment about *you*, often you can find the most satisfaction and fulfillment in helping others! Read the book *The Go Giver* by Bob Burg and John David Mann.

Use the My Contributions Blueprint Worksheet.

WWW.MYLIFEDESIGNBLUEPRINT.COM/BLUEPRINTS

Remember, find something that matters to you!

Health & Fitness

I want to remind everyone reading this that I am not a subject matter expert on every single section of this blueprint. I am simply sharing what worked wonders for me in the hopes that it can work wonders for you. I hope that, through this book, I will be able to connect with others who are, in fact, subject matter experts in these different areas and that, through collaboration and discussion, they can help me to improve this Life Design Blueprint process. I will then share a revised version with those of you who wish to stay connected to this ever-growing and expanding system for designing your life.

In this section, I track the meals I eat and how much water I've consumed during the day, as well as when I take my vitamins. It gives me a reference point to look at, and I have seen great results with just tracking this.

You can also track your weight in this section. However, I list my weight as one of my habits in the progress and tracking section.

What other health metrics matter to you? Keep those things here.

You can include recipe ideas you want to try. An amazing and cost-effective service I've used is called emeals. It basically gives you different types of meal plans for you to choose from, with the related recipes to make these tasty meals. It breaks down the recipes into a grocery shopping list that I then use to save time and effort by grocery shopping online. All you need to do is pick it up at a scheduled time. Many grocery outlets now offer this kind of service.

No more dragging hungry kids to the grocery store trying to find things on opposite sides of the store.

Keep any ideas or articles you find valuable that pertain to health or fitness in this section as well.

YOUR HEALTH IS YOUR WEALTH

Think about how many people have all the money and time in the world, but they don't have the ability to enjoy any of it due to poor health. If your health is weak and you have major complications, you will know the truth of this statement. Taking care of yourself is so important, but we often take for granted the incredibly complex things our body has to do to keep us alive. When you neglect or fail to take care of your own health and wellness, you are writing a bad check that will bounce one day, and the price could be your life or your quality of life.

Overwhelming evidence makes it clear that nutrition plays a major part in many diseases and disorders. The foods we eat and the substances and chemicals we are exposed to absolutely have a direct effect on our health. Anyone who tells you otherwise is likely trying to sell you a product that is harmful to your health.

Things we take for granted like toothpaste contain highly toxic chemicals. Yet we don't even think twice about putting them into our bodies because we assume that those products are not causing us any immediate harm.

I actually switched to a natural toothpaste with neem that contains no fluoride. While people still argue about whether fluoride is safe, when a truck full of fluoride flips over, people in hazmat suits have to come and clean it up. Anyone who wants to tell me that putting that in my mouth is safe I find hard to trust.

Virtually all products that come into contact with our body such as body wash, shampoos, detergents and soaps all have an effect on us. Whenever possible, I seek out healthier alternatives to mainstream products that are being mass marketed to us.

The main point I want to make is that you should stop assuming that because something is sold in a store or you see it on TV, that means that it's safe. You would be appalled if you researched some of the products that you have casually been allowing to pass into your bodies and those of your children.

With economic pressures to remain profitable, it is not always in a company's best interest to fully inform the public or even do the right thing when it comes to long-term health. This is not because companies are inherently evil. This is the result of the way businesses are structured. They are often beholden to stockholders and investors.

Here are just a few of the various health subjects that got me thinking more about what I put in my body.

- Processed foods
- The marketing of junk foods to children
- Food producers minimizing health concerns associated with their products
- Foods labeled healthy aren't necessarily healthy
- Fluoridation of water
- Magnesium deficiency in most adults
- Genetically modified foods
- The effects of aluminum in deodorants
- Vitamins and supplements

Your health is critically important. Yet, there are lobbying groups that actually fight against anti-obesity campaigns aimed at informing people about the real risks of obesity. The ones who stand to lose most are those who fight these types of initiatives.

Relationships

If you asked thousands of people in the very last years of their lives what truly matters in life, most would say relationships. This may seem like old wisdom and somewhat common sense, yet we wait till much later in our lives to truly value our relationships.

I do not just mean romantic relationships. I mean your relationships with your family, friends, your parents, your children, your peers at work, your boss. Human beings are social creatures and with the advent of the internet and mobile device technology, we have never been more connected. Yet, I would argue that we are, in some ways, less connected and more isolated now as a result of "social" technologies. People barely even look at each other in passing. Couples out to dinner sit at restaurant tables with their noses buried in their cell phones and only look up to eat.

Families don't eat dinner together. The TV and taxing work schedules take time away from actually interacting. How many of us have sat at a table with a group of people where over half of them were lost in the cell phone zombie scroll? That's what I call wasting your life, scrolling through social media. The irony is that you are in a social situation surrounded by actual people you can interact with, yet many choose to retreat and stare into a tiny glowing 5-inch screen to see what other people in other places are doing. This prevents people from being present in the moment, making them practically zombified.

Do an experiment for yourself. Start to look around and notice how other people interact with each other. Watch people driving to work on the freeway with a cell phone shoved in their face, not even looking at where they are driving. This used to outrage me. Now, I just get as far away from them as possible.

I have literally counted dozens of people on a single stretch of freeway that did not look up from their phones for 10 seconds or more. At 70 MPH, you are traveling at around 105 feet per second, which means in 10 seconds you covered 1,050 feet, all without ever looking up from that cell phone. A lot can happen in 1,000 feet traveling at 70 MPH. You can end your own life or kill a whole family, all because you were mindlessly scrolling on Facebook or Instagram.

This is not a technology problem, in my opinion. This is a personal and relationship problem. People do not value others. They do not value being present in the moment. We have become detached from our own realities through technology and blame that technology. The blame lies with us. We have to consciously make the effort to be more present where we are. I used to say, "I'm going to be where I'm at" when someone asked me where I was going as a sarcastic response. Yet, whenever I arrived at where I was going, what would I do? I would retreat into my tiny screen just like so many others still do. This is being bred into our younger generations and, in my opinion, will increasingly become a larger problem unless we have a mental and emotional shift in our values.

BE WHERE YOU ARE

I want to challenge anyone reading to stop spending so much time doing the zombie scroll. By the way, this is not actually your fault. It has been compared to the addictiveness of smoking cigarettes in that there is a release of chemical endorphins in our brains while using social media.

This makes it become a habitual action that we derive some sense of pleasure from, yet the more this becomes a habit, the more we become detached from our present moments. The actual happiness and enjoyment in our physical lives starts to decrease, leading us into a downward emotional spiral without even noticing.

You may be at work and bored out of your mind, so you decide to scroll through Facebook looking at how many of your friends are on vacation enjoying their lives. Now you're wishing you were not stuck in your cubicle listening to people that you can't stand.

This is a bad place to be. Try to limit your social media and phone use to specific times in your day and otherwise put your phone on "do not disturb," especially if you are working with others. As with any habit, the key is to not try to stop it entirely through sheer willpower. Your willpower will deplete and you will revert back to doing the same thing as before. The key is to replace it with something better. So, when you get the urge to scroll through Facebook, find something else to do instead. This will help you to overcome that negative habit.

PEOPLE WHO CAN BE PRESENT AND ENGAGE WITH OTHERS WILL LEAD

If you can be present and focus on the moment you are currently living, then you have the ability to effectively lead yourself toward achieving the things that are most important to you. Some of the benefits of being present can include:

- Improving your personal and professional relationships
- Getting more done in less time
- Feeling more peace of mind
- Feeling more enjoyment
- Achieving your dreams and goals
- Observing opportunities you previously missed
- Feeling more energy throughout your day
- Making more money

This idea of being present can help you in almost every aspect of your life. However, in the area of relationships, its effects are significant.

Paying attention and being in the moment with others is one aspect of building successful relationships. Attention is in such short supply, yet when full attention is given to others, the connection that can form is astounding. When someone sees and feels that they have your full attention, that is when a connection can be formed.

DESIGNING YOUR RELATIONSHIPS

In this section of your Life Design Blueprint, keep ideas and ways to improve your personal and professional relationships.

Reminders of important dates.

- Birthdays
- Anniversaries
- Other people's interests

The *5 Love Languages* is a great book that provides some deep insights into why romantic relationships can seem dysfunctional and how to truly reach people's hearts.

Imagine trying to speak Chinese to someone who only speaks

Russian. All too often, this is how we attempt to communicate love to others. I highly recommend reading this book. It's very short and the insights you will gain into your own relationship failures or successes will be powerfully realized.

RELATIONSHIPS WITH YOUR CHILDREN OR FAMILY

Ask yourself these questions regularly.

How can you spend more quality time with your family?

- Plan a family reunion
- Camping trip
- Go to the beach
- Trip to Disneyland. Use the Travel Plan Blueprint from earlier.

PROFESSIONAL RELATIONSHIPS

In this section, keep ideas and ways to improve your professional relationships.

Keep reminders of important dates. This works professionally too! People are all just *people*! We tend to view people we work with in a different light.

- Birthdays
- Anniversaries
- Other people's interests
- Goals
- Type of work they do

Make a commitment to reach out to one new person a week. You could have 52 new contacts at the end of a year. If you did one per day, that would jump to 365. That's quite a few people. A popular phrase comes to mind: your network is your net worth!

Connecting with people can lead to possibilities that you never imagined.

Ideas & Mind Maps

Mind maps are, in my opinion, an incredible way to write out thoughts, notes and ideas in a visual way that works the same way our brains are wired to work.

Tony Buzan popularized the term *mind mapping*. However, it has been around for some time, dating all the way back to the 3rd century.

Mind mapping has *revolutionized* my ability to think and act strategically. It was like a holy grail when I discovered it. I cannot overstate how helpful and useful mind mapping has been for me. Without mind mapping, this book and many of my successful ventures would not have been possible. While mind mapping is mostly thought of as a handwritten form of brainstorming and mapping things out, I prefer to use digital mind maps.

DIGITAL MIND MAPPING

Mindmeister is my favorite mind mapping app. However, there are many mind mapping applications. I prefer digital mind maps because I can never run out of room as I would when my piece of paper or whiteboard space is filled. Another major benefit for me is the ability to work on my mind maps from any device and from anywhere. I may have been brainstorming some ideas the night before, and while leaving a meeting, some new idea pops into my head. If I was using handwritten mind maps, chances are I would not be able to immediately plug this into my mind map. You can also collaborate with others and work on mind maps together, which for me has been a brainpower multiplier. Having multiple minds brainstorming and working on a single mind map gives you the power of multiple brains that form different connections that you otherwise would not see. This, in itself, has been invaluable for me personally in my business and in the businesses of my clients. It seems like such a simple concept, yet once you experience the power of this form of visually connected externalized thinking, you will wonder what on earth you did before you discovered this incredibly useful tool. At least, that's how I feel about it.

The applications for mind mapping are limited only by your creativity.

It helps me to:

- Structure ideas
- Make complex plans
- Retain information
- Write content
- Organize my life
- Achieve my strategic goals
- Solve complex problems
- Make passive income
- Help others to simplify situations
- Generate ideas
- Clear my mind

BRAIN DUMPS AND EXTERNALIZING

Our brains are super complex organs made up of billions of neural connections that control every function in our bodies. Our brains control our perception, motor function control, motivation, learning and memory, just to name a few. It stands to reason that at any given time, there is a tremendous amount of activity going on in our brains. The ever-changing daily reality we are faced with does not seem to be slowing down anytime soon.

With all of the tasks and to-dos we need to accomplish in a single day and all the things we forget or fail to do that add up over time, our brains become filled with these things. It is important to externalize and take out of your mind all of the numerous tasks, ideas, desires, goals and needs, and record them in another form. By removing them from our mind and putting them in a written or digital form, we allow our brains more capacity to think and solve problems more effectively.

Bestselling author and productivity consultant David Allen makes some simple yet profound observations. He says, "Your mind is for having ideas, not holding them."

"Externalizing your thoughts and ideas frees up your mind to do what it does best," he writes.

He has also observed: "Much of the stress that people feel doesn't come from having too much to do. It comes from not finishing what they've started."

This I can personally attest to. As a serial entrepreneur and lifelong learner, I have been plagued for much of my adult life with having too many open or unfinished projects. Before learning about externalization, I was keeping everything in my mind and in very limited written form. It was not until I took the time to move all of it from my brain onto paper that I freed myself up to actually complete more and more of the projects.

Brain dumping and externalizing should be easy and simple. It can include mind mapping, writing in a journal or notebook, or just entering your thoughts and ideas into a note-taking app like Evernote. The point is to get it out of your head and onto paper or in digital form, so that you can free your brain up to actually take action on some of those ideas and thoughts.

KEY TAKEAWAYS

You now should have a good understanding of the following.

- All the different sections of your Life Design Blueprint
- What goes in each section of your blueprint
- Ideas that will help you to design your life

ONE KEY TO EFFECTIVELY USING YOUR LIFE DESIGN BLUEPRINT

Create a habit of using your Life Design Blueprint at least two times per day, in the morning and in the evening. Remember, experts say it takes 61 days to form a new habit.

8

How Do You Use Your Life Design Blueprint?

Now that you understand all the sections in your Life Design Blueprint, I want to discuss how you can actually use all of this in reality. I will start by sharing my process and ideas for how you can use yours. The point is to make this entire process yours. There are some key aspects to the Life Design Blueprint that are critical to its effectiveness that I will quickly outline below.

THE LIFE DESIGN BLUEPRINT PROCESS

- Externalize your goals outside of your mind
- Decide what you want and why you want it
- Envision your desired outcome
- Plan backwards from the result you want in detail
- Create habits that support those goals
- Track the progress of those created habits
- Review frequently and make adjustments as needed
- Act on the plans you create

- Enjoy the process and making progress
- Reframe failures to be constructive to your growth

This is a simplified approach to a more complex interdependent system that I have created. Just remember something that has taken me many years to learn: if you focus on survival, then that is what you will get. You will just barely make it and survive. If you place your focus on being prosperous and living an abundant life, then that too is what you will get. You almost certainly will not live a prosperous and abundant life if you are always focused on just getting by.

Here is my recommended process for using your Life Design Blueprint

Go through the sections briefly in the morning. The excuse of not having the time is irrelevant, a bad habit and not the truth. If you had to spend 15 minutes a day for the next month to get a million dollars direct-deposited to your bank account every year for the next 20 years, then 90% of you would find a way to make it happen.

If the exact kind of life you desire, the one you will have carefully designed and planned with your Life Design Blueprint, does not excite you and motivate you to spend 15–30 minutes each day to make it happen, then there is another underlying issue. Your designed life is not compelling enough; perhaps you have picked goals that are not as important as you thought them to be.

CHECK YOUR OWN BS

Another major cause for this is your own BS, otherwise known as your belief system. What you believe to be possible for your life will often very closely frame what you will be able to achieve. The top performers in the world in their respective fields seem to have at least one thing in common if you look closely. They have a very high belief in themselves and the possibilities for their lives. Not all of them started this way, however. It is possible for you to acquire this ability and skill. Your belief system is one of the key factors that will determine to what heights you can climb.

FORMING THE HABIT

Set aside 15–30 minutes a day to look over your Life Design Blueprint.

- This is probably the most critical habit you can form.
- It makes all the other things in the Life Design Blueprint automatic.
- If you focus on this one habit, you will, by design, achieve stellar results.

Remember, tracking progress toward your goals is *fun* and inspiring. It will give you an incredible sense of accomplishment as you see and feel actual results and progress.

IMPORTANT NOTE

Some sections may matter more than others to you personally. However, keep in mind the process outlined earlier in this chapter. You cannot skip any of those major steps and expect to make rapid progress. Make this process yours. I am merely providing the framework that has created tremendous results for me in my life.

The second most important aspect to all of this is reviewing your week and tracking your wins and lessons learned. This step is non-negotiable. If you do not regularly review what your results were for the week and take the time to plan how you will adjust moving forward, then you may find yourself lost and far from your intended destination by the time you look up to realize you're off track.

IT'S REALLY SIMPLE

Pick one day to review your week. I use Sundays as my review, reflection and planning day. I spend at least one hour going over my week and planning the next one.

DON'T BE DISCOURAGED IF YOU MISS DAYS

The point is not to be 100% robotically perfect. The point is to set goals and track progress while making it a game and reviewing your experiences regularly. If you miss a day, pick it up the next day. For the habit tracker, put an "O" in that day's box for the habit you missed. Review why or what caused you to miss that day. Make sure to take note of this so that you can be aware and readjust moving forward. Remember, there is no losing, only learning! You can always reframe your point of view to make a negative "loss" into a valuable growth opportunity.

One of the daily habits I track is whether I went over my Life Design Blueprint in the morning and at night. This is one of my keystone habits. If I did the rest of the process correctly, then I will be guaranteed to be making forward progress on my goals.

I love seeing my habit tracker full of X's. It's become a game for me. I have made this into something fun that I get great enjoyment out of. To see and chart my progress in forming relevant and successful habits is an amazing process.

TRACK ALL YOUR WINS!

Every time you accomplish something, write it down in the weekly goal setting and review blueprint. I have also included a Monthly Wins

Blueprint to add up all of your progress from the weeks at the end of your month.

FIND THE MONTHLY WINS BLUEPRINT.

WWW.MYLIFEDESIGNBLUEPRINT.COM/BLUEPRINTS

At the end of each week during your review, you will see how much you have accomplished. Over the course of a month, those will continue to add up and create massive momentum and a feeling of excitement every morning when you wake up. I believe this is because you're making actual and continual progress toward things that truly matter to you.

TRACK AND REFRAME YOUR FAILURES

This is just as important, if not more important, as keeping track of your wins. We have a tendency to want to avoid failure. We want to avoid talking about our failures, thinking or dwelling on them. We gain such an aversion to failure that we eventually stop trying anything we deem to be too difficult for us to accomplish in the short term because of the chance of possible failure. Failure feels bad; that's why we avoid it.

THIS IS THE DIFFERENCE BETWEEN THE LIFE YOU WANT AND THE LIFE YOU WILL GET

As I talked about early in this book, you and I have been programed to fear failure. We have been conditioned first genetically through evolution, when failure once meant life and death for us, and secondly through the public education system and most common parenting tactics. We simply were not equipped to handle failure constructively for this day and age. I want you to begin to reframe your ideas about failure.

FAILURE IS THE MOTHER OF SUCCESS

The most successful people on this planet understand that failure is actually a key determining factor for success. Rapid failure, review and adjustments will show you precisely what you need to change and adjust in order to be successful.

MASSIVELY SUCCESSFUL FAILURES

Thomas Edison

It has been reported that Thomas Edison tried over 1,000 times unsuccessfully to invent the lightbulb, each time beginning more intelligently than the last.

Harrison Ford

Ford struggled for many years as an actor, only getting uncredited acting roles. He worked as a carpenter and was hired to build cabinets at the home of the famous director George Lucas, who recognized his talent and cast him in a supporting role, which later led to him auditioning for *Star Wars*. The rest is history.

JK Rowling

Her manuscript for what would become the wildly successful Harry Potter books and eventually the films based on those books was rejected 12 times by major publishers. The franchise has sold over 400 million copies and is one of the bestselling series of books in history.

Oprah Winfrey

Oprah was fired from her first television job. Her boss told her she was too emotional and not right for television. Without this failure, Oprah may have never become the first black female billionaire.

Colonel Sanders

Harland Sanders worked for decades in various jobs, including fire-fighting, insurance and sales. He pitched his fried chicken recipe over 1,000 times to investors and was rejected. At the age of 68, he found a buyer and started to franchise his Kentucky Fried Chicken business.

Henry Ford

Ford failed numerous times and went bankrupt five times before founding the successful Ford Motor Company.

Albert Einstein

One of the world's greatest minds, Albert Einstein was not able to speak until he was four years old and could not read until he was seven. He was expelled from school and was refused admittance to Zurich Polytechnic School. He later changed the world with his discoveries in physics.

Michael Jordan

Considered one of the greatest basketball players of all time, Jordan was cut from his first high school basketball team. He missed more than 9,000 shots in his career and lost close to 300 games. On 26 occasions, he lost the game by missing the very last critical shot. A famous Michael Jordan quote is: "I have failed over and over and over again in my life, that is why I succeed."

USE THE FAILURE BLUEPRINT YOU CAN FIND HERE.

WWW.MYLIFEDESIGNBLUEPRINT.COM/BLUEPRINTS

MAKE THIS A GAME

Have fun with this. The point of living, in my opinion, is not to arrive. The point is to enjoy the process of getting there and the person you will become while doing it.

Turn this entire process of checking off your habits that you completed for the day into a game. Make tracking progress something enjoyable.

It sounds simple. Yet, once you experience and feel the excitement that you will get from making progress, you won't want to live your life any other way. You can become addicted to making measurable progress, and I would say that this is a great addiction to have.

Think about this. You may not understand how to reach your goal this week or in the next month. However, with careful mapping, you will be amazed at how much you will have accomplished after only a few months following this process. Imagine being able to track, measure and see all the progress you made over a year?

Use your Life Design Blueprint for the year and, at the end of the year, you will *marvel* at how far you have come. Do the same review process for all of your months at year's end and make your adjustments and plans for the upcoming year.

Looking over just my first month of 2017, what I have been able to accomplish by using my Life Design Blueprint has blown me away. My first quarter has been a major breakthrough in my own life, and I know the rest of 2017 will be the very best year of my life.

I *sincerely* and genuinely hope that your Life Design Blueprint does even more for you than it has for me!

9

My Most Successful Habits

MORNING MEDITATION

I will be honest. I thought meditation was weird before I understood it. Curiosity about what Buddhists actually believe took me down the infamous YouTube rabbit hole.

This rabbit hole led me to trying meditation.

I have always had an *overactive* and over thinking mind. It never stops working.

I couldn't sleep many nights due to being overly excited or stressed out about something.

I saw a video of a man who had lived as a successful college professor and ended up becoming a Buddhist monk. He explained the basics of meditation. After the first time you are able to feel calmness of mind, you will cry tears you cannot control, he said. They will not be tears of sadness or angst, but just a massive release, he explained.

I mocked the idea that I was going to cry sitting cross-legged like a Buddha statue.

By the third time I tried to meditate, I felt an *intense* release of pressure in my mind.

I felt a calmness and connectedness to *everything* around me. My mind was finally quiet!

My eyes were leaking profusely, and I felt incredible joy and peace! I laughed as the tears I could not control continued to come down.

I was alarmed by this yet amazed at the same time. I later became obsessed with chasing that intense yet peaceful calm feeling again. I learned later on there was more to meditation than this feeling, but nonetheless, meditation has *changed* my life for the better. The benefits in my life are *priceless*!

Here are some easy ways to learn and try meditation.

The apps: Headspace and Calm offer a great way to try guided meditations for a free trial period.

I started with free guided meditation videos on YouTube.

MIND MAPPING

I mind map *everything*! No joke! It creates clarity and helps me to think more effectively. Without mind mapping, this book wouldn't even be possible for me personally.

- Mind map your life's goals for the year. I will include a free template of this.
- Mind map your week. This is my favorite way to plan my week.
- Mind map books. I retain so much more from what I read and can revisit info quickly. I have mind maps of popular books on my blog.

USING MY LIFE DESIGN BLUEPRINT

- I have already discussed why and what this has helped me to accomplish.

- It truly has revolutionized my effectiveness, focus, commitment, achievement, feeling of happiness and progress.

I accomplished in record time goals I thought would take many months.

TRAFFIC UNIVERSITY

I listen to audiobooks in the car while in traffic. Before I discovered meditation, this helped calm my mind while driving.

Traffic was once the bane of my existence and the single largest waste of time that drove me to absolute madness.

Using this time to *learn* has transformed my life and added so much value into my life. Major problems have been solved and major money has been made due to simply listening to audiobooks in my car.

I also:

- Listen to audiobooks while working out in the morning.
- Listen to audiobooks at 1.5x speed, sometimes 2x speed. It becomes normal and I start to process things faster. Listening on regular speed is almost painful now.
- I get through audio books in half the time.
- I often go back and mind map from audiobooks in the evening.

NO MORE ROAD RAGE FOR ME. I'm learning something valuable. Therefore, my time is not being wasted by rude people on the road anymore.

SENDING LOVE TO OTHERS AND THINKING ABOUT GRATITUDE

Focusing on others and sending them good thoughts or wishing them well takes the focus off of you and creates a very powerful residual effect in your life.

I make it a habit right after my meditation to send good thoughts to a few people in my life, even people I may not like very much.

I look over my gratitude list briefly and pick a few things to focus on for a few moments that I am grateful for. This has created a great sense of satisfaction and happiness for me personally.

This also works for me in traffic.

I started trying it out on rude people on the road whenever someone cut me off. I started to hope they would be happy and have a good day. It would quickly end the feeling of frustration. I can't explain how or why this works. I will only share with you that it works. I get to keep my high energy mood and keep on learning from my audiobook.

READING WITH A PURPOSE

I became a truly committed and avid reader when I read the book *The 7 Habits of Highly Effective People*. I used just one thing I learned from it to transform a very toxic personal relationship. The issues were quickly resolved and the situation was made better than I could have ever imagined. It led to getting my daughter back in my life. This immediately sold me on the massive benefits of reading.

After reading 70 books in one year, I made a discovery. When I had a very specific purpose in mind for why I was reading something, I retained and was able to put what I read into practice.

I came across one of the most arrogant, self-centered, know-it-all individuals I've ever met in my life. This person would literally tell everyone how much better he was than everyone else at everything.

It was unbearable for many people around him. I nearly threw in the towel and ran away. Instead, I found a book called *How to Deal with People You Can't Stand* and figured out how to cope with the situation. I made serious connections through this experience and other events transpired because of my reading this book.

SERIOUS FOCUS WITH TIME-BLOCKING

I use a method called time-blocking to focus on singular tasks. I learned this from Gary Keller in his bestselling book *The One Thing*.

Because I use my Life Design Blueprint and mind mapping, I plan my actions out in steps before I start something and can focus on *one* thing at a time.

I put on ambient focus music and just get into a deep focus and get to work.

This was never possible for me until recently.

I never leave Facebook windows open while working on my computer.

I check email only at certain intervals and times.

I also put my iPhone on "do not disturb."

It is very rare that you absolutely need to react and respond right away to anything.

I get back to people quickly and am able to be extremely productive and blast through complex tasks in my day.

At the end of my day, I am often very proud now of what I have been able to accomplish. I used to let tons of distractions take me off track, and I would feel serious guilt about it.

SOME VALUABLE SHIFTS I MADE

After hearing that the most successful people read, on average, 60 books in one year, I set the goal of reading 60 books in 2016. I ended up reading 70 books, with my new goal of mind mapping 200 books in 2017.

Here are just 10 of the books that made a major impact in my life in no particular order.

- The One Thing by Gary Keller
- The Compound Effect by Darren Hardy
- The 7 Habits of Highly Effective People by Stephen Covey
- Failing Forward by John C Maxwell
- The Magic of thinking big by David J. Schwartz
- The secrets of the millionaire mind by T. Harv Eker
- Money master the game by Tony Robbins
- Awaken the giant within by Tony Robbins
- Rich dad poor dad Robert Kiyosaki
- The virgin way by Richard Branson

10
Lessons Learned & Takeaways

Nothing is created only once. Everything is created three times.

- In the mind
- On paper
- In reality
- Ensure your habits are leading you to achieve your goals.
  - Choose the right habits that will put your goals on autopilot.
  - You don't choose your future. You choose your habits and they choose your future.
- Design your life with the endgame in mind.
  - Gain power and confidence over your life by designing it.
- Progress builds momentum and gives life meaning.
  - Tracking victories and progress makes you feel excited and creates momentum.
- How to stay committed to your intentions.

- o Build small habits that domino into larger changes into your life.
- How to kill procrastination.
  - o Manage and block out your time and effort. Deliberately making a plan makes it easier to get done.
  - o Know why you want or need to do something.
- Get rid of confusion and create clarity in your life.
  - o Clearly see where you are and where you want to go.
  - o Track progress daily.
  - o Review your actual actions.
  - o Make constant weekly corrections and observations.
  - o Creates incredible clarity of purpose and direction.
- You learned some of my secrets and habits that can lead to massive progress.
- How I use my Life Design Blueprint.
- 10 key takeaways from five top self-development books that transformed my life.

You learned how to break down and design your Life Design Blueprint, and I gave you a good starting point to design your very own.

NOW IT IS YOUR TURN TO START BEING A MASTER DESIGNER OF YOUR OWN LIFE!

You are infinitely powerful and can create and attain the life you have always desired. Choose to show up and live out that inner greatness I know that dwells within you.

I cannot wait to hear all about your stories of success and triumph through applying and using this system!

Be sure to join our Private Mastermind Group on Facebook by visiting:

MYLIFEDESIGNBLUEPRINT.COM/PRIVATE-MASTERMIND-GROUP/

And lastly remember that for everything you want you have to pay the price.

About the Author

ALBERT POLANCO serves as one of the spearheads of marketing strategy for Crucible Strategic, based in Houston, Texas. With a background in filmmaking and internet marketing to numerous entrepreneurial pursuits, he has garnered over a decade of hands-on expertise and has helped numerous clients cultivate strategies that turn a mediocre company into a force to be reckoned with.

To date, Albert has owned a number of lucrative companies, including an Internet marketing agency and a video production company. In addition, he was a multiple-time marketing director in the automotive industry.

Currently, Albert serves as the Co-founder of Crucible Strategic along with his business partner Ryan Reed who served together with Albert in the United States Marine Corps.

No matter what venture he takes on, Albert strives to elevate people's minds and awaken them to their limitless potential so they can shoot for the stars. Ultimately, he aims to make a positive impact by serving others and leaving a legacy for generations to come. He is laser focused in helping others who yearn for lasting abundance through proven tools and insight that yield the highest possible returns.

Outside of his career, Albert Polanco is an avid reader (he reads 100+ non-fiction books every year on average) and technology enthusiast.

He also likes meditating, learning new things, and everything pertaining to outer space.

How to Connect with Albert

Listen to The Crucible Strategic Podcast available on iTunes, Google Play Music & Stitcher.

WWW.CRUCIBLESTRATEGIC.COM/PODCAST

For Business Inquiries
albert@cruciblestrategic.com

Made in the USA
San Bernardino, CA
15 July 2017